JUNGLE
ESCAPE

JUNGLE
ESCAPE

by
Ed and Doreen Dulka

WEC PUBLICATIONS
Gerrards Cross, Buck. SL9 8SZ England

CHRISTIAN • LITERATURE • CRUSADE
Fort Washington, Pennsylvania 19034

CHRISTIAN LITERATURE CRUSADE

U.S.A.
P.O. Box 1449, Fort Washington, PA 19034

BRITAIN
51 The Dean, Alresford, Hants SO24 9BJ

Published jointly with

WEC PUBLICATIONS
Bulstrode, Gerrards Cross, Bucks. SL9 8SZ,
England

British Library Cataloguing-in-Publication Data.
A catalogue record for this book is available from
the British Library.

Copyright ©1992 Ed and Doreen Dulka

CLC/USA ISBN 0-87508-092-8

WEC ISBN 0 900828 53 6

Cover photo: Superstock / W.Woodworth

This book is also obtainable from
WEC International
P.O. Box 1707, Fort Washington, PA 19034.

PRINTED IN THE UNITED STATES OF AMERICA

CONTENTS

CANOEING WITH CANDIDO

andido's left arm shot out ahead of him and the fingers on his hand flipped in unison as he directed the boat over to the left of a strong current. He moved his head constantly from side to side and his eyes darted across the turbulent water as he sought out a path that would keep us clear of rocks while we passed through the rapids. He sat erect in the front of a 27-foot log crafted into a canoe, with his legs extended forward in the narrowing confines of the prow. Candido (cán-di-do) was an Indian of the Cubéo tribe. He was our guide for the trip.

Reading the movement of Candido's fingers, Cesar, Candido's son-in-law, tended the motor in the rear of the canoe. The canoe was tossed and buffeted in the swirling waters of the rapids, but we slowly made our way up the river.

The center of the boat was filled with

gasoline, our baggage (food for our trip, personal belongings and Welthy's dental tools), and Welthy and me! I think perhaps *we* were the most cumbersome pieces of baggage, as far as our Indian guides were concerned. In front of us lay Candido's personal possessions, his bag, machete and shotgun. The bag was an old flour sack which had been dipped in crude rubber mixed with powdered sulphur, to give it a water-proofing seal. It had turned black with age and had cracks in the rubber from its constant use. The rubber-coated bag was a sign that he had been a collector of crude rubber in his youth, a prestigious job in that older era.

Candido was typical of the Cubéo tribe in appearance, except that he had a mustache, an uncommon feature among most Indians. (To those who live with them for any length of time there are easily recognized distinctive features in each tribe, and we had contacts with eight different tribes.) Candido was barrel-chested and appeared to be in robust health. His shirt and pants were neat, if not meticulous. He was a man who was proud and accustomed to being respected. In just a few short days our future would be set by this man, who was always in command of the things around him. As the years passed, we saw him continue in that role.

As a new missionary with WEC International, I was accompanying Welthy Key (our resident missionary for many years among the Cubéo Indians) on a survey trip among the Carapana people, to see how we could best establish a church-planting ministry there. Welthy had been with the Cubéos for many years, having originally pioneered the area with another missionary couple. She was fluent in the language and was not only a preacher but also a dentist. This amazing lady was greatly respected by all the Cubéo Indians. A regular participant and a dominant figure in the church life, her influence meant that we, too, were readily accepted by the Cubéo—and that in turn provided a stepping-stone to the Carapanas. Welthy was a great source of encouragement to us.

My wife Doreen and I had just recently arrived in Bogotá with our three small children. They were waiting there now for the results of this survey which would determine the location of our next home.

In the southeastern corner of Colombia, in South America, lies the Vaupés River, a headwater to the mighty Amazon River. It is less than one degree off the equator and shimmers in tropical heat. Mitú (me-toó), on the banks of this great river, is the capital of the Vaupés (vow-péz) province, which takes its name from

the river. To arrive at Mitú from "civilization" involves a three-hour flight in a cargo
plane, using your own luggage as a seat.
The plane either dodges the tropical thun-
derstorms or has to bump through them.
Either way, it is an exciting flight. Mitú is
the hub of all activity in the Vaupés, and
the connecting point with civilization. It is
the commercial center for all the Indians
of the area, and a crossroads for those
going into the jungle for one reason or
another. I was using it as a launching pad
to take the gospel to the Carapana Indians.

The Carapanas' (car-ah-páwn-ah) territory bordered Cubéo (coo-báy-oh) Indian
territory which surrounded Mitú. The
Cubéos had had missionaries for nearly
twenty years, but the Carapanas had only
had passing encounters with the gospel,
through occasional visits from missionaries or Cubéo Christians. They had always
been very resistant to the message; but
now, through Wycliffe Bible Translators
(WBT) who were translating the Bible into
Carapana, we heard that the people were
becoming more responsive. The WBT
couple, Ron and Lois Metzger, were eager
for us to make a start in church planting.
In this jungle we would experience for ourselves the wonder of watching God change
the hearts of men.

The jungle reached right down to the

river like a solid green wall, over whose top an unending blue sky stretched with drifting puffs of cloud. Vines and small trees protruded out of the wall, trying to grasp the sunlight. Large trees leaned out for sunlight too, until the river cut under their roots and toppled them into the water. Every few miles the jungle wall was broken by a village clearing. The trees would be cut away and a grassy area of one to five acres would be dotted by thatched-roof houses. Each house would be ringed by a barren spot where the grass had been cleared away to keep undesirable insects and reptiles at a distance.

The day wore on, and the sun burned hotter as it shone from above and reflected off the water and the bottom of the canoe. It was difficult for me to remain so inactive. My eyes took in the river and the jungle around me, storing impressions and sights that soon would become a part of my life. It all seemed so big and endless.

We turned the canoe into a creek that fed into the Vaupés. There we got out, stretched our legs, and ate our dinner of sardines and crackers. Both of these items came in sealed tins which thankfully were waterproof. No time was wasted, and as soon as dinner was over we set off again. Before long we came to Mirití (mir-e-téa), the longest rapids (perhaps three quarters of a mile) that we would encounter in our travels. Its length made it very nerve-grinding. We bounced backward and forward, seemingly making no progress as the swift waters swirled around us. Candido's arms shot up, first on one side then on the other, as he directed our way up through the currents, between rocks that were not visible but were dangerously close to the water's surface.

When we reached the end of the rapids, we were abreast of a large, very neat village. It had many houses, and a school building which was directly behind a neatly trimmed basketball court. But the village was quickly out of sight as we rounded the bend, and we returned to the jungle with its monotonous river-to-sky green wall.

The wind and the sun on the river had cracked my lips and burned my skin. The clouds continued to float by as if in no hurry, but somehow never getting between the sun and my drying body. Bend after bend, the river looked the same. A boat passed heading the other direction. Then in front of us loomed an island, and we took the passage to the left of it. The Indians had told me that at the far end of the island we would find rapids called "the whirlpool."

I was wary of this "whirlpool," because on this stretch of river there was no place where the canoe could dock, allowing most of the passengers to walk around the rapids while the experienced canoists negotiated the whirlpool. However, it turned out to be much tamer than I expected, and I relaxed my muscles with a sigh of relief. The village where we were to spend the night was now only an hour away—but I wondered if I could stick it out! Candido, however, had been sitting rigidly at the helm all day, and only a few times had he shifted his weight. His attention was riveted on the river ahead, as though he saw things we couldn't.

The hour passed. The village finally peeked into view, tucked just around the bend on the left. The noise of the motor had already attracted a crowd of people, and when it became apparent that we were going to stop, more people came to the bank. Candido and Welthy were instantly recognized and joy showed on the Indians' faces as a sign of their welcome. The chief of this Cubéo Christian village was a long-time friend of Welthy's. Candido stepped lithely from the canoe as it touched the bank, while I stood up and tried to straighten my legs—and wobbled over and around the luggage. We shook hands with everybody. The village chief told Welthy where we would be staying and the people all moved in that direction. I took one look at the slippery mud bank and decided I could not climb it twice, so I turned back to pick up my baggage before making the ascent.

At the top of the bank I heard loud, concerned voices and saw four men kneeling around something on the ground. Candido was talking to them, and in a few minutes the men stood up and lifted what turned out to be a young boy from the ground. Welthy stopped and spoke to them, and then Candido came to sit on the bench beside me, his face showing real concern. The boy had had an epileptic seizure—his first. The men around him were all elders of the church, and their instructive teaching had been to lay hands on him to pray while they held his thrashing body down. I hadn't seen this kind of faith in the U.S.A., and I wondered if I really had what it took to work among these Indians. Would I be able to bring the Carapanas to the mature faith I had seen in these Cubéos?

Eight years later, as we prepared to flee from the Communist guerrillas, we would know the answer to that question.

"Don't be saddened by what is taking place. Remember I told you that this might happen. You know that we came here purposely to plant a church among you. You and I believe that you, Biviano, are ca-

pable of carrying it on now," I would re-mind him.

"Yes," he would reply before I had a chance go on, "Yes, we will carry on the church."

Welthy and I ate alone while Candido and Cesar joined the Indians of the village. Welthy usually ate with the villagers, but she was taking into consideration my "American stomach." Immediately after supper we hurried to clean up for the evening service, a common event in every Christian village. My Bible was deep in my pack so I decided not to bother to dig it out, especially as they would be reading and speaking in Cubéo and not in Spanish.

The light source was a candle on the table at the head of the room. On one side of the table was the congregation. The opposite side of the table had a single bench where the elders sat. The chief of the village asked if I cared to sit with the elders. I really did not want to, but neither did I want to offend them, so I sat up front.

The service began with singing in both Spanish and Cubéo. Most of what was going on was beyond me, so I relaxed and my mind began to wander. Soon they were reading in their Cubéo Bible. The book, chapter, and verse had been given in Spanish but the reading was in Cubéo. The tiring day caught up with me and I drifted back to my daydreaming. Then reality crept through the fog as I heard my name repeated. All eyes were upon me! What? I was being asked to speak!? My mind reeled. I did not have the slightest idea what they had read, nor was I fluent in Spanish. Worst of all I did not even have a Bible. I looked imploringly to Welthy. She told me it would be a good opportunity, but she did not push me. I decided that this would be as good a time as any to start, so I borrowed Welthy's Bible. The Indians sang another hymn while I quickly read through the passage in Spanish. It was not even a passage that I was familiar with! I asked God for His guidance and then shared from His Word. When I finished I was both surprised and pleased. God had taught me in a few minutes that if I would do the work He had sent me to do, He would enable me. And this lesson was to be repeated over and over as we obeyed the call God had given us . . . to prepare the Carapana Indians for ministry to their own people.

Waking up in the gray dawn in a Christian village came to be a joy to me. Somewhere in the village one person would start a hymn or chorus, then voice by voice, other people would join in as they roused from sleep. After two or three songs, one person in each house would begin to pray. When one had finished another would pray until everyone in the house had committed the day to the Lord.

When prayers were over that morning, I rolled out of my hammock and strolled out of the house toward the riverbank. Some of the men were coming in with their early morning catch of fish. They told me the name of each type of fish they had caught, first in Spanish and then in their own Cubéo. I remembered neither. Welthy passed the morning distributing medicines and extracting teeth that were rotten and painful. While she did this, we loaded the canoe for another day of arduous river travel up the Vaupés. And then we left.

At noon I noticed splotches of foam floating in the water. I pointed them out to Candido and he told me that they came from the rapids ahead. We passed two more long bends in the river and then we saw a mountain looming close to the water, coming right down to the river in a long slope. On the other side of the river the mountain sloped up once again. Each bank protruded into the river with large outcroppings of rocks; the Vaupés River was squeezed between the two sides of the mountain, and tumbled down over the rocks to form the rapids. On a hill on the right side was a village called Mandí.

As we neared the rapids I could not take my eyes off them. In a 250 to 300-yard course the river dropped five-and-a-half feet, greatly increasing its speed. We turned below the rapids and docked the canoe. Candido directed Welthy and me to get out of the canoe and walk around through the village while he and Cesar took the canoe through the rapids. I inwardly breathed a sigh of relief. Cesar and Candido backed out into the river again. I watched transfixed as the water rushed at the canoe. The motor started and they directed the sturdy craft headlong into the rapids. The boiling, tumultuous water tossed the long boat around like a cork. It bobbed back and forth and Candido searched out a path which, though invisible, would take them through the areas of least resistance. Cesar followed the directions of Candido's outstretched arm with the flicking fingers which said, "Over more, over more." When they reached the middle of the rapids all forward motion seemed to stop! They just sat there in the middle of the rushing water. After what seemed an eternity to me I noticed that little by little they were moving up river, and then the canoe seemed to lurch forward again. It cleared the rapids and I scurried off to catch up with Welthy and be ready when the canoe docked.

Little did I know then that this apparently friendly village would later be considered our last obstacle as we escaped from the Communist guerrillas. I would be taking the canoe down through the rapids alone while Doreen and the children walked rapidly through the pro-Communist village, praying not to be detained by them.

After we left the rapids the villages diminished in frequency. Many were entirely hidden from view so it was only a wisp of thin smoke or a barking dog that betrayed their presence. The afternoon wore on with the same drying wind and burning sun as the day before. There was a brief shower, but the nearly constant glare of the sun and water hurt my eyes. There were no more rapids to look forward to, no special landmarks to anticipate, and nothing more to learn from scrutinizing the jungle wall. As the day wore on into late afternoon the only change was a cooler sun.

At last we rounded a bend and had a complete change of view. There before us was a mountain that sloped down to the river. It had two lovely rounded twin peaks. It seemed even more delightful when the Indians told me that just this side of the ridge was the Caño Ti (Caño—pronounced cá-nyo—meaning "creek" or "stream"). The Caño Ti was the waterway into Carapana territory. My heart beat faster. What would I find there? Would this be the place of our ministry?

As I contemplated these things we reached the mouth of the Ti and turned into it. The lush jungle immediately gave way to a type of scrub brush which for half of its life is flooded with ten to twelve feet of water. It looked ugly. The water was very dark brown. After traveling for about forty-five minutes, we came to a village. We docked the canoe with great expectancy, but found that these people were not Carapanas but Cubéos! Also, they were in the process of repairing their longhouse and did not have room for us to stay the night. It was getting dark, so they suggested a Carapana village close by where we could probably stay.

On the way to that village we saw a man sitting in a small canoe fishing, and we waved to each other. Eventually we came to the village and asked permission to stay the night, only to find that the man we had passed on the way up was the chief of this village. We would have to wait for his return to obtain permission to stay. When he arrived thirty minutes later it was dark, but he gave us a place to lodge. His name was Biviano (bi-vi-á-no). Ron Metzger had told me that he was a Christian.

The sounds of chirping birds awakened me just before the loud racket of nearby monkeys drowned out all other jungle sounds. It had been a cold night. The place we were given to sleep had no walls, only a roof. During the night it had rained, so the chill and dampness had crept into my blanket. As I looked out from my hammock everything seemed dark and ugly. The people themselves were not friendly—in fact they looked wild, as though they had just walked out of the jungle.

After breakfast we had a service and the villagers took great interest in learning new Christian songs. Candido preached, then Welthy, and then I shared that my family and I were looking for a village to live in where we could preach and teach the gospel.

We ate lunch before heading upriver to visit the other villages and approach them with our proposal.

The visit gave much first-hand knowledge of Satan's hold on these people, as I observed the paint on their bodies which was supposed to ward off evil spirits, and saw one of their "fiestas"—a loose form of satanic worship and an orgy.

On the way back down the Caño Ti we decided to paddle a while as we were running low on gasoline. Without the roar of the motor we were able to hold a conversation to a background of the sweet notes of jungle birds. Candido told us about his conversations with the different villagers. He was excited as he related his visit with one village chief, adding that as far as he knew, it was the first time that the man had accepted gospel literature. There he was—working again! That Candido! I was frustrated! He was doing the missionary work, while I was tongue-tied with my limited Spanish. Candido, like most South American Indians, spoke some Spanish besides his native tongue, and usually another dialect or two. I was able to observe, though, and the lessons I learned were important. If Candido, a Cubéo Indian, could be a church elder and a missionary, couldn't the Carapana Indians also be taught to be effective witnesses for Christ? They could be a viable force to reach both their own people and the many tribes to the south which had even less contact with the gospel. Candido would be a good role model to keep in mind as we worked towards making Carapana disciples.

When we arrived back at Biviano's village, I spent the afternoon walking around the clearing of no more than five acres. The "village" consisted of only one Indian longhouse (occupied by all the resident Indians) and the 15-by-30-foot roof under which we were staying. There were two docks; one was well used, the other unused, and near it was the remains of an old house. There were two paths that led off into the jungle, and although they were inviting I was not ready to wander off yet. As I looked around—dismal describes the place—I felt very depressed, a feeling which is not normal to my nature. I was also experiencing a tug at my mind.

"God," I said, "my family and I have already been refused entry by a village on another river that seemed so lovely. Now here I am in this place and it seems so ugly and depressing. You must make it clear, very clear that You want us here."

My gaze drifted along the riverbank and there I spotted a snowy egret, looking uncommonly white in these surroundings. It looked out of place, but at the same time my heart felt a communication from God: "God wants His pureness here!"

My eyes opened wide in wonder, at such a clear impression from God. I prayed, "Is this a sign from You, Lord?"

Later that night as I strolled along the path to the unused dock I looked up into a full moon, and stood in its brilliant reflection. Again the same communication came to me as earlier in the day. "God wants His pureness here!" While still in the presence of that Peace, the first thing I saw was a spotless white flower, something like a jack-in-the-pulpit. Again it was impressed on my mind, "I will make

My pureness to shine in this place."

As I turned in for the night I confessed, "Lord, I don't like it here, but if the villagers invite us back, we will come."

In the morning we had a service during which much time was spent in learning new hymns. Afterwards I approached Biviano and told him of our desire to come and preach the gospel to the Carapana Indians and to live here in his village to teach him and his people the Bible. I also handed him a letter written to him by Ron Metzger in Biviano's own language. The letter outlined our reasons for wanting to come and also listed the possible pressures they might have to face in having a foreigner living there with them. It took them all of forty-five minutes to read the one-page letter. There was no immediate response and I did not want to push them. Candido took up the conversation in Cubéo and I did not understand what was being said. I went out of the house to stretch my legs after the long morning service.

Just as Candido had lifted his arm and directed the canoe through the rapids, taking full responsibility for the canoe, he now began to take authority in this situation. His voice came floating to me out of the Indians' house. Little did I know that as a lawyer presents his case before court, Candido was presenting our case before this people. After a short time I returned to the house and sat down again. Finally, when there was a lull in the conversation, I broke in and presented our proposals again, asking if they would have us. Things had already been arranged! They had agreed to have us come and live with them and teach them the Bible. I was overjoyed! My mind then raced ahead to all of the plans we had made. I asked them when it would be convenient to them for me to bring my family, and that too had already been discussed. Biviano had said that he had two weeks of work waiting before he could begin to build us a house. I was amazed. So soon? I could not be ready to come back for at least four weeks.

Candido was very pleased with the proceedings, and in the midst of it all he asked if the village had a name. Since it had only an Indian name—Pamopetá (pa-mo-pe-tá), meaning "Beach of the Armadillo"—he promptly christened it Nazareth, a good Biblical name.

On the trip back to Mitú, I began to learn how we had been accepted at Nazareth. Candido, an elder of the Cubéo church, was the one who taught catechism lessons to new converts. Seven years earlier Biviano had wandered into a Christian Indian conference, heard the gospel and had received Jesus Christ as his personal Savior. He was taught and baptized by Candido and was like his spiritual son. Candido's suggestion that Biviano accept us was therefore a powerful one. Candido had also thrown in a package deal, saying that we would also bring in trade goods to supply the needs of the people of the river.

Who but God could have given us Candido as the guide for our trip? Only God knew the influential role he would play in our being accepted in the place God had prepared for us. Who but Candido, my barrel-chested friend, would have seen the need to help me put across our desire to serve God among the Carapana people while looking after the welfare of one of his own spiritual children at the same time?

I had more than a "sneaking suspicion" that God had arranged it all. I only hoped that I would be worthy of the call and as ready to serve as I had seen Candido serve all who came into contact with him.

NAZARETH, HERE WE COME

Ed will be telling most of the account, but once in a while there will be friends that I would like to tell you about. So you will be hearing from me from time to time.

We had just spent four hectic weeks of buying, packing, shipping—and we had prayed a lot too! Now we were on our way to our new home and ministry. Our party consisted of Welthy Key, Ed, myself, our three children (Amy, 5; Eddie, 3; and Becky, only six months), and a motorman called Saul who handled the canoe.

We had been traveling most of one day already. It was a long day, starting with the packing of the canoe and then sitting for hours with the three children while Ed was squeezed in the back with the motorman (who ran the outboard motor). Hours of sitting in the boiling sun and then being soaked by the rain . . . a short lunch . . . wet diapers . . . and cramped, wiggling children on canoe seats was not my idea of a good day. This was our first trip into the jungle as a family, and Ed was hoping and praying that we would all like the jungle and share his sense of adventure. However, he was over-optimistic! I was looking at the river and thinking, "It's so big"; and then at the children, "They're so small." The terrifying rapids were the worst parts of the journey. I kept wondering which of the children I should try to save if the canoe over-turned! If I grabbed the baby, could the other two kick enough to stay afloat a while at least? Surely we would lose the few possessions we'd been able to bring along with us to set up a home.

At last we made our first night's stop in this strange new life together. We had pulled in at a Cubéo Indian village, one that Welthy hadn't been to before, but it had turned dark and we had no choice but to ask for housing. All traveling is done by river, and all Indian villages have a central house where they let travelers stay. It is just a thatched roof and poles with no walls. If you personally know someone in the village, however, they will usually invite you to stay at their home.

Cooking over an open fire was not

bad, but trying to bed the children down in hammocks and tucking mosquito nets around them was another thing. I was never good at tying knots, and invariably someone would fall out of the hammock. The many watching eyes of the Indian women and children made my ineptness that night very humbling indeed.

"Ahhh! We're all tucked in at last—settled for the night. Thank You, Lord, for helping me today," I sighed at last.

But before long . . . "Mom," called Amy, "I need the bathroom"—echoed immediately by Eddie. I found the flashlight, which I'd tucked into my hammock, unwrapped the mosquito net and lurched to the ground. I located the three pairs of shoes which would be needed for the trip and unwound the children's nets.

We headed outside into the jungle night. It was dark—oh so dark! Real bathrooms were unknown here, so we just went down a path leading out of the village into the edge of the jungle. Something moved along the path! I wanted to scream! Instead we hurried back into the house to wake up Ed. As the four of us stumbled down the path together, Ed laughed, "If only our folks at home could see us now!"

Finally, I got to sleep . . . only to be wakened by Welthy, calling my name. "Doreen, there's a young man standing over my hammock staring at me."

"What do you want me to do?" I asked. "Pray," she whispered, and started talking to the young man in Cubéo. I didn't understand what she was saying, but I certainly prayed. At last she called out to say that the man had gone, and I fell wearily asleep. The next day, Welthy shared with me that she had been very conscious of an evil presence in the village, and had spent most of the night in prayer.

Our second day was just like the first—only longer! It was the beginning of the wet season and we were constantly drenched with rain. That night we stopped at a Cubéo Christian village, and Ed informed me that this was where the boy had had the epileptic seizure. Welthy seemed much more relaxed and said it was the nicest village around. To me it looked the same. The thatched huts were the same, and so were the people—except for their eyes. There was a brightness in them which had been absent in those of the villagers where we'd spent the first night. Thankfully, we settled down. Welthy fell into a sound sleep but we, who were still getting used to hammocks, tossed and turned all night.

Day three was still wet—but as we sheltered under our plastics we felt more enthusiastic because this was the day that we expected to reach our final destination, Nazareth, and to start the work to which God had called us when we were teenagers. It was also our seventh wedding anniversary! It had taken us seven long years to get here—including Bible school, WEC International candidate course, and Spanish language school.

We huddled under our plastic covers all morning, then late in the afternoon the canoe turned into a smaller river, the Caño Ti, and within forty-five minutes we docked at a village where we were greeted by a large crowd of enthusiastic Indians. This was Nazareth, our new Carapana home.

FIRST IMPRESSIONS

Getting out of the canoe, I tried to smile and say "Hello" in Cubéo, as Welthy had taught me, but the words just would not come. The men looked so primitive and dirty. They wore some clothing, but their overall appearance made the television Tarzan look tame!

I turned to the women for reassurance, but their toothless faces, their long, matted hair and the filthy children clinging to them were almost my undoing. I had asked God to give me a love for these people, and a peace that we were in the right place—and I had neither.

Ed badly wanted me to see the people

in the villages and to love them as he did—but when I met them my only impression was "They're so dirty!" This wasn't the way Ed wanted me to react at all.

Ed was really surprised by the large welcoming committee and their warmth when we arrived at Nazareth. I, too, was overwhelmed by our reception, and in turn gathered our children close to me to protect them from all the reaching hands that were trying to pat and touch their little blond heads. Blinking back tears, I looked around to see what all the excited chatter was about.

Biviano, the village chief, was talking to Ed and Welthy and showing them a thatch-roof shelter with a bark floor, but no walls.

"Oh well," I said, "we've spent the last two nights in similar huts, so one more night with a bark floor and no walls will be okay."

Ed turned and looked at me oddly. "Honey," he said, "this isn't for one night. This is your new home." Ed was moved by the efforts the villagers had made to build our home. The bark floor had been finished only that afternoon, and that was why so many people were there. They were proudly waiting to show us their work. I went through the rest of the evening in a state of shock.

"Lord," I thought aloud, "I've given up everything to follow You. Is this really what I've been praying and preparing for all these years?"

When we unloaded the canoe, the Indians formed a line from the river and began to pass the items along, fingering each one with many "Ohs" and "Ahs." They'd never seen most of the things before, so Ed explained what each one was. I was at the house, trying to place the items in some sort of order as they arrived.

Once the children were settled and the canoe emptied, Ed started rummaging among our belongings. "Happy anniversary," he said, hugging and kissing me as he presented me with a package. Welthy was quite impressed at his thoughtfulness, but I just wanted to cry. I wanted him to feel as I felt: that God was being unfair in asking us to live among these people. I opened the package; four new coffee cups for our new home and new beginning. Then Ed took me along the river path for a walk and, stopping, put his arms around me and held me for a long time. He did know how I felt, and even so he loved me very much. This was where God had called us and this is where we would stay until God told us to leave.

The next three days flew by in a whirl. Welthy taught us many practical things about life in the village: how to trade items for food, comparative prices, and the dos and don'ts of Indian life. Then she announced that she was leaving the next morning, to get back to her own area . . . and said that we would do just fine! We waved her off the next day with tight throats, realizing just how far we were from anything that was familiar. We had nagging feelings that there were some things we hadn't been taught in Bible school!

ON OUR OWN

The first few days of adjusting were rough. With only a roof and a floor, we were visible to everyone all the time, and they would wander in and out, touching everything they could see.

We all had to make adjustments—physically as well as mentally. Becky's stomach reacted to the boiled river water (which was all we had). We were eaten alive by gnats and mosquitos during the day. They bit any uncovered area, so we dressed in socks, long pants and long-sleeved tops—and then got unbearably hot in temperatures over ninety degrees.

I kept Becky in her playpen, with a mosquito net over her day and night. In the first four weeks we used up all the insect repellent we had brought for four years! When we discovered that there were fewer insects at night, we took off our extra clothes at dusk . . . only to uncover other bites: sand fleas love covered places, especially the areas under tight waist bands and under the arms. Many nights were spent bathing down small bodies with water and baking soda. The only small comfort offered to us was that in time our bodies would be more resistant!

During the first few weeks walls were put up around half of our house, and this became our kitchen, dining room and bedroom. We soon copied the Indians' method of taking down the hammocks during the day to make more living space.

For a long time I despaired of ever being able to get into a hammock easily and staying there: one night I swung in and straight out onto the floor on the other side. Another time Ed slung my hammock above Amy's; as soon as I stretched out, a rope came loose and I fell down, taking Amy and her hammock with me. Mercifully, only my pride was hurt!

I'd like to tell how much I witnessed for the Lord that first month, but I have to confess that it was a matter of sheer survival day by day. Paul's words in Philippians 4:11, "For I have learned, in whatsoever state I am, therewith to be content," gradually became a reality to us.

We had a church service every evening at seven. Some incidents are funny to recollect, but they reduced me to tears at the time. In their own houses, the Indians just squat on their haunches or sit on a stool about eight inches high. I was always offered a stool, but couldn't balance on it. Sometimes I missed it altogether and tumbled onto the floor. Other times, just as I was about to make a safe landing, the child in my arms would squirm, throwing me off balance, and we would both fall in a humiliating heap. One evening during our first week, a bug flew down inside my blouse, making me jump up involuntarily in the middle of the service. Everyone laughed—except me!

PAULINA OFFERS A HAND OF LOVE

The glowing highlight of my first days in the jungle was a relationship I developed with a woman called Paulina. She could not speak Spanish and I could not speak a word of her language, but a real friendship started one memorable morning. I was frustrated to the point of tears from struggling to get a fire going in order to cook the family's breakfast, when Paulina came over and gently pushed me out of the way. She put twigs in the place where I was trying to light the fire, then lit them with a burning branch she had brought. The fire immediately jumped to life, and from then on Paulina always seemed to be on hand to rescue me.

One day, while the baby was asleep, I took Amy and Eddie to the river with me to wash clothes. It was impossible to do this and keep the children safe at the same time, but suddenly Paulina appeared and, slipping off her dress, took Amy and Eddie to play in the river while I scrubbed clothes. This became a daily ritual, and while we were at the river's edge she also showed us what was safe and what was dangerous. It became fun to watch her point to one berry which was good to eat and another which was harmful. We learned the Carapana words for "good" and "no," and within days were asking Paulina many questions by pointing at things and saying "Good?" She never tired of answering "Yes" or "No." Many evenings when I was trying to make our evening meal, with the children acting fretful and the baby crying, Paulina would come in. Picking up Becky (who always stopped crying when Paulina was around) she would take Amy and Eddie by the hand and walk outside with them. This, too, became a daily ritual.

Talking to Paulina one day, through an interpreter, I learned that she was waiting for her family to come and collect her. She was a relative of Biviano's wife, Emilia, and after many years of marriage her husband was sending her back to her own family because she had borne him no children. She showed no bitterness about this, and her attitude was always one of love. Her one great fear was of snakes. She told me of a poisonous bite she had suffered years before, and how her leg still ached from it. She often asked for medicine for it, and had a constant horror of being bitten again.

Paulina came down with hepatitis and became very weak, lying in her hammock for five days without eating. The children and I missed her so much. Gradually she began to recover, and as soon as she could sit up in her hammock, I would sit beside her and show her picture books produced by the Wycliffe translators—trying to learn the Carapana words for each item. We had great fun at my attempts to pronounce the Carapana words in the book. During those mornings together, as I tried to learn Carapana, I taught Paulina to count in Spanish. She could then find the numbers in the hymn book during our evening service, and was proud of her accomplishment. Paulina had heard the Word of God while living in the village with us. The service each night had been translated for those who did not speak Spanish. I was not able to tell through our sign language conversations whether or not she was trusting Jesus as her Savior, but I knew that she had heard the message of salvation.

One day, during her long recovery, I was feeling discouraged to the point of giving up. Amy, Ed and I had also come down with hepatitis. Paulina came walking into my house and handed me a wild orchid. "Dora nuña," she said. "Doreen is good." A lovely compliment.

Very soon after that, her family came through on their way to Mitú and said they would be collecting Paulina on their return trip a week later to take her back to their village. During that week she asked me if she could take some books with her, so I gave her one of the Bibles and a hymn book that we always used at the evening services. I was satisfied that she already knew she was taking our love and prayers, but now in the gift of the Bible she had something tangible.

On the day she left, she brought her nephew with her to say good-bye. She had the Bible in her hand and she opened it, handing it to her nephew who read a passage in fluent Spanish. Paulina beamed. She patted the Bible, said it was good, and then asked me to write her name in it. When I had done that, she asked me to put my name under hers. I did so—and then came the time for her to go.

There were tears in my eyes as she left, but my heart told me it was right for Paulina. In the six months that she had been my friend she had taught me how to adapt to jungle life. She had also taught me that behind a dirty face and toothless grin there was a real, caring person. I thanked God for His love for these people, knowing that because of His precious provision for me I could love them too. Paulina had reached out to me, and God had used her to help me adjust to the call He had given us to reach the Carapanas.

SCHOOLING—FOR US ALL

When Amy was almost six, I started her schooling, using correspondence courses and trying to fit her into my daily schedule when I had time. I quickly learned that children learn better in the earlier part of the day, and also in a set routine. Lessons were fun, and a new experience for both of us; but as the months rolled by I kept thinking of all the other jobs that desperately needed my attention. Then Amy's attitude to schooling soured, and with an unwilling pupil it was no longer fun to teach. She became rebellious: none of the other children in the village had to go to school, so why should she? All the preparation needed for correspondence school lessons was no easy task for me either. I had to study a lot each day.

By this time the village had "grown." In particular there were Luisa and her children. They had come to the village for a New Year's party, and had just stayed on and settled in. Luisa had lost her husband three years earlier when he was bitten by a coral snake. She had eight children. The fifth child was a thirteen-year-old girl named Ameria.

Another distant relative had arrived with his two boys and two infant children. One of the few "drifters" among the Indians, the father would move with his family into a village and then stay for as long as they were tolerated! The older boy, Joachin, who was twelve, and Maciliano, eight, could not move on fast enough, as far as I was concerned. They were both badly behaved, foul-mouthed Indians—the worst we had ever met. This was because their father had never practiced, nor taught them, normal Indian cultural behavior.

Mischievous as he was, there was still something likeable about Maciliano, who began following Ed around wherever he went. Biviano took a liking to both the boys, and decided to teach them more acceptable ways. During garden-cutting time he showed the boys how to make a garden from scratch—as well as getting some free labor from them in the process. The Indian system is to cut out all the underbrush with a machete, then fell the large jungle trees and let them dry. When they are dry they are all burned, to provide ash for fertilizer. The method is known as slash-and-burn.

When it was time to cut down the large trees, Ed, Biviano, his sons, and Joachin and Maciliano went along to help. The idea is to cut each tree half way through, without allowing it to topple over. When an acre or more of trees is ready, one man goes to the edge of the area, all the others leave, and he fells one tree completely—so that it topples all the others, like dominoes. The first day of the work, when they had prepared about an acre of trees, Maciliano cut one too deep and it toppled. Six men scrambled for their lives, and thankfully not one was hit. Maciliano did not go back to the garden work after that!

With so many children now in the village, Biviano one day asked Ed if I could teach their children too. We discussed the idea, but I knew I could not fit them in with Amy as they were too illiterate. I had taken a course in teaching illiterates to read, however, and thought this could be a ministry for me, so I decided to give it a try. The Indians worked in their gardens all morning, not returning till one o'clock. After a small meal, they were ready for their next activity, so I started classes at two o'clock in the small schoolroom they had built onto our house.

I was not prepared for the enrollment.

Everyone in the village came to class. The women sat in the front and men at the back. The Laubach course I used provided charts that were big enough for all to see. We started in.

"This is the letter 'a,' it says the sound 'ahh,'" I told them. "Everyone say 'ahh'!" "Ahh," they replied.

"This is the letter 'e.' It says, 'ehh.' Say 'ehh.'" And on we went through the Spanish alphabet.

For these classes I had learned the right statements and questions in the Carapana language, and now used them repeatedly. After we had covered about twenty letters, the older women lost interest and dropped out. Biviano stayed for some weeks, but mostly to keep order and to make sure that his own children learned. Eventually the class dwindled to thirteen students, two of whom already knew how to read. We also learned numbers, so that they could find the right hymns in the song book, as Paulina had done. Ameria, one of Luisa's daughters, was the quickest with numbers.

The workload was getting heavy, and my days were really full with teaching Amy every morning and the other students every afternoon. Three-year-old Eddie roamed back and forth between Ed and me, while Amy and Becky stayed with me as I taught. I was still cooking over an open fire, carrying water from the river, doing the daily laundry, caring for the children—and quickly becoming exhausted!

LEARNING TO TRUST IN TRIALS

Each day seemed to bring renewed attacks from Satan. Some were very subtle, and some were blatant.

By now I had a small wringer washer; on one of our trips to Bogotá to obtain our resident visas we had bought a gasoline-powered washer to take back with us. While I was washing one day, I scooped up a pile of clothes which I had sorted and put them into the washer, and everything seemed to be fine. When the load was done, I put my hand into the soapy water and felt something I couldn't identify. Pulling it out, I found myself clutching a drowned scaly green lizard. I screamed! When the shock had worn off, I started again; this time I put the clothes in piece by piece with a stick!

Another night I was washing the dishes after the evening meal—knowing I would be too tired to do it after the evening service which had already started. I worked my way through the pile, then began wiping the counter. Picking up the kerosene lamp in order to wipe underneath it, I was confronted by a large black scorpion with its tail poised ready to strike. I grabbed the fly swatter and struck twice, but the scorpion escaped through a crack in the bark wall. That incident led to a recurring nightmare that a scorpion had crawled into the children's beds. I couldn't sleep again until I'd been up to check on them. It seemed that Satan was using the natural elements of the jungle to put fear into our hearts.

A final incident led us to pray much more specifically—and desperately—for God's protection. One stormy night a terrible electrical storm was crashing around us. The children were already sound asleep and Ed and I had just gone to bed when there was a terrifying crack of lightning. Sparks flew all over just outside our bedroom wall and we could see them through the cracks in the bark. We jumped up and peeped out, only to see a palm tree on fire less than fifteen yards away. Ed went off to check on the children, who were still asleep! As he came back, another bolt struck even nearer, and we just clung to each other—praying to God to help us overcome our fears.

I fell asleep, and God gave me a vision of our house as if I were seeing it from the air. I looked down and saw a white light over the house. It was in the shape of a cross, and the intersection was right over our bedrooms. At each end of the cross was an angel—protecting the house. The next day I came across a card a dear friend had once given me. It read, "The will of God will never lead you where the grace of God cannot keep you." I thanked God for showing me how to trust Him. From that point we never doubted that our lives were in His hands. Although we became sick from time to time, and faced many dangers, there were no incidents, major or minor, that Ed or I could not handle with God's help.

That same week I found another encouraging verse in my belongings.

The light of God surrounds me,
The love of God enfolds me,
The power of God protects me,
The presence of God watches over me,
Wherever I am, God is.

BACK TO SCHOOL

School with the Indians was becoming tedious. Joachin and Maciliano tried all sorts of tricks and rude noises to break the concentration of the class. And no matter how hard I tried, I could never get anyone to read aloud. Maciliano announced one day that ours wasn't a real school anyway, because they did not have to pay to attend.

One day I became so furious with Joachin and Maciliano that I walked out of the class to the room where Ed was, and told him that I would never teach those two again. "You take them and teach them," I cried.

Ed sat them down at the kitchen table with a primer written in Cubéo. He ran through the sounds with them, then read them a story about a rat. He could pronounce the words, even though he himself didn't know what they meant! But the boys' eyes lit up as they heard the story in their own language. He showed them the pictures which went with the words, and they were now eager to learn. Realizing that the sounds together made words, they were quickly reading themselves. When they had finished the story, Maciliano looked very accusingly at Ed and muttered something in his own language. Ed asked him to say it in Spanish. Maciliano then called Ed a faker! He naturally assumed that if Ed could read the Cubéo words from a book, then he must also be able to speak Cubéo and understand it!

The two boys were always at the evening services and listened intently. But that didn't mean they were not mischievous. However, it wasn't our place to correct them; Biviano took that responsibility on himself—and he was more tolerant than we were. They did hear the gospel time after time, I'm happy to say, and gradually their vulgar talk and bad habits began to drop off.

Luis and Alberto, Biviano's sons, slightly older than Joachin and Maciliano, made a definite profession of faith, and their influence helped to bring the others into line. When she was fourteen, Ameria, Luisa's daughter, became a Christian, and the joy of the Lord was very evident in her face. Biviano was pleased that these young people had been converted, and he especially doted on Ameria. He made sure that she understood the translation of the message each night, and showed her other privileges. He also took on the unspoken responsibility for her family, since her father was dead.

About this time we became aware of something unusual which had taken place. The jungle around us which had been so dark and oppressive was now a pleasant place and seemed to have an abundance of light. Visitors who came to our village would remark on its loveliness. Ed and I smiled at each other, for we had guessed the reason. Christ, the Light of the World, now had dominion in this place where for thousands of years Satan had reigned, keeping these people in dark bondage. Jesus had come to be praised!

GOD SENDS AMERIA

The day finally came when I could not get out of bed, having succumbed to total exhaustion. I lay in bed for three days while Ed did all the household chores, the teaching, and his own work too. At the end of the second day, Ed came and sat on the bed, saying that it was crazy for me to try to keep up with this punishing schedule. He asked if I would consider hiring Ameria to work for us. She was only fourteen, but she was bright. Yet I groaned inwardly as I thought of how much it would take to teach her about household matters. Another job! I realized, however, that Ed was right. I knew he was trying to help, so I agreed.

Ameria learned quickly and became irreplaceable. She fitted into the family like a big sister, and also taught me many easier and quicker ways to do my own jobs. I had brought from Bogotá a straw broom, which was much too soft for our floor. Ameria spent her free time one afternoon measuring and cutting pieces of vine, and the next day arrived with a broom made of woven vines. I doubted its usefulness, but on the split-palm floor it was able to get down in the cracks and do an excellent job.

We also learned about new foods from Ameria. She knew many ways of cooking plantains, a type of banana which cannot be eaten raw. We had always fried them, but Ameria boiled them, made them into a drink, put them in soup, cooked them with beans, sprinkled them with brown sugar—and even made them into chips! She was immaculately clean, so I could rely on her to do the washing and have a meal ready each day when I had finished teaching Amy. She also took care of Becky, and did as much house cleaning as time allowed.

I valued her most when it came to cleaning and preparing wild game! The hair had to be singed off and the animal gutted. This was part of the Indian woman's work, but I just could not tackle it. I tried once when Ed was away, but I'd looked so miserable that Biviano had sent his son over to finish the job for me. Fish was much easier, and Ed soon had Eddie and Amy trained to do that job quite nicely.

There were some things, of course, which were quite difficult for Ameria to learn, and we had some blunders. When these incidents occurred we would correct them, then sit down and laugh together. Not long after she had started to help us we had fried fish, and I'd used newspaper to absorb the grease as I took the fish out of the pan. When Ameria washed the dishes, she took the pieces of newspaper, gently washed them, and hung them up to dry!

She was the first local young person to have access to a motor. Granted, it was only the two-horsepower motor of our washing machine, but to use it was a privilege that few had. The boys would stand around in awe as she started up the motor and began to work. They eagerly asked her to let them pull the rope, and spent so much time watching her that eventually they knew every step by heart. One day, after I thought Ameria had "mastered" the machine, while I was teaching Amy it stopped working. I assumed it was out of gas, but was sure Ameria knew what to do, so I kept on teaching. I heard her in the gas shed, and soon she was pulling on the rope to start the machine. Nothing happened, and it was some time before I realized that something had gone wrong. As I went out I got a forlorn look from Ameria. I checked the tank. It was full. I pulled the rope. Nothing happened. Alberto came over, and I asked him to pull the rope, but he shook his head. He said he didn't think the machine liked the kind of gas Ameria had put in. I checked the tank, and he was right. It was kerosene instead of gasoline!

Ameria filled the void which Paulina had left and gave me companionship; and she also became Ed's language informant. He often asked her how to pronounce Carapana words, and tried them out first on her. Many times God used the Indians to help us practically as we helped them to find Christ and operate as His church in the jungle. We eventually learned to live from the jungle, and copied Indian ways of cooking and eating. Later, when the time came to flee into the jungle from Communist guerrillas, we knew we could survive, for God had prepared us.

Many summer afternoons we would paddle the canoe to a sandbar and enjoy the sun and the sand together while Ed and Eddie fished in a deep hole nearby. One day while there, Ameria taught us to cook the potato-like manioc root in a fire in the sand. We dug a hole, lit a fire in it, and when the wood was glowing, put the manioc root in the middle. Then we covered it with green leaves and filled the hole with sand. While Ed was catching bigger fish we caught minnows with a net, and Ameria began to gut each one individually. When she had about twenty, she made a sheath for them using a palm leaf. She informed us that she would need one leaf for each person, so we tried to help her. As we handed our efforts to Ameria, she patiently rewraped each clutch of fish properly. Then she built another fire over the buried manioc and made a rack of green branches over the fire, laying the minnow cobs on the rack. While our meal was cooking, we all went for a swim.

Soon everyone was hungry and ready for our minnow cobs and manioc. Ed,

Ameria, our children, and the Indian school children we'd brought along with us were soon starting into this delicacy. I unrolled the end of my minnow cob, all hungry and ready to enjoy this meal in the great outdoors. I picked out a minnow. It was staring at me! I turned it around in my fingers and took a bite from the other end. I moved my jaws a few times in a chewing motion, but it was no good; I tried to swallow, but it wouldn't go down. Every eye was on me, but I just couldn't do it! I passed my minnow cob on to Ed, but the children begged to have it. Next I peeled my substitute potato with enthusiasm. This had to be good, I told myself! I eagerly bit into it, but instead of the baked potato with butter of my imagination it was something only vaguely resembling a potato—edible but slightly sandy. My American stomach still had adjustments to make.

On the next trip we took, I realized that I was not the only one with adjustment problems. I had decided that I was not going to starve on a day's outing. Even if I had to feed the whole Indian neighborhood, I was taking along something palatable! I packed a large bowl of tuna-and-noodle salad, bread and butter, cookies and Kool-aid. When it was time to eat, Ed dished up bowls of salad, and put a piece of bread and butter on each plate. What a treat!

When everyone was seated and we had given thanks, all eyes turned to a young fellow named Miguel. He took one sip of Kool-aid. His eyes dilated, and he promptly spat it out, putting the glass down as if it contained poison. Next he dabbed his finger in the butter, grimaced and declared it greasy. Another fellow next to him offered to eat it. Finally came the tuna salad. We told them it was fish, their favorite food, and Miguel pioneered again. He took a large spoonful and closed his mouth over it. His taste buds registered that the Kool-aid had been mild compared with this, and he rushed over to the river to spit it out, his face making the weirdest contortions.

I pretended not to notice as the other children followed Miguel's example, and came to the conclusion that one person learning to eat Indian style was better than making a lot of people miserable trying to eat American style. Over the years I did, however, offer the Indians some new things that could be grown locally and bought cheaply. Some of them were accepted, and popcorn was the all-time favorite!

CHILDREN GIVE A HAND

Alberto, Biviano's youngest son, was a mischievous thirteen-year-old when we first arrived at his father's village. He had no fear of us, as the other children had, so he was given an unusual assignment: Biviano assigned him to keep an eye on me until I got used to jungle life . . . but to do it discreetly. He did. After a few weeks in the village, however, I decided to take one of the paths and see more of the jungle. I was careful to keep to a well-marked path but I'd gone less than five hundred yards when I saw Alberto wandering along casually behind me. He gave a vague reply when I asked him what he was doing, and kept right on just strolling nearby for the rest of my outing. This happened for a whole year—until Biviano was satisfied that I had enough knowledge of the jungle not to perish if I was left on my own!

Once I realized what was going on, I

often invited Alberto to come with me, or let him know where I was going and what I was looking for. Alberto was always curious to know what I was up to, and he was very knowledgeable and informative. Most of the time, though, he would let me blunder through on some hunch of my own without intervening. Alberto was one of God's special gifts to us, more than we realized at first, for not only did he initiate me into jungle life, later he was to be invaluable in helping us escape from the Communist guerrillas.

We needed to carve out land from the forest and plant our own garden, but I realized we could not have it too close to the house or it would attract ants and the village chickens. I picked out what I thought was a suitable site, and at the first opportunity Doreen, the children, Alberto and I went down near the riverside to make a start. The site was on quite a high hill above the river, so we had to make steps down to the water. It was also overgrown with trees, but we found four which were not too large and felled them to let the sunlight in. Next we cut away the six-inch-high roots which covered the ground, and when it was clear and exposed I pulled out my American seeds and planted them in neat rows. Our experimental plot was ten feet by ten feet, but it took the entire morning to prepare.

We were quite sure that soon we would have all the vegetables we needed. Alberto, however, had very definite misgivings, though he had never said a word during the whole ludicrous procedure. At that point I hadn't had the opportunity to observe their slash-and-burn form of agriculture, and did not understand it's importance. The ground was virtually sterile, having no topsoil, and the trees sapped all the nutrients. Not a single seed sprouted! It was only then that Alberto ventured to suggest that we would need to clear a large section of jungle and burn the trees to provide fertilizer. Together we cut a new section, and step by step he patiently showed me how to make a real jungle garden.

Alberto's dedication to us went far beyond his father's imposition. He was always around . . . and we soon became close friends. He had a tender heart and was one of the first to follow Christ as his personal Savior, never missing a church service. He could read, and soon got to know all the hymns and choruses. We had obtained various records from Gospel Recordings Inc.—made in the local dialects—and whenever we had visitors in the village Alberto would bring a record from the meeting room and play it. Soon there would be a crowd around him, and usually all the villagers would be quiet so that even from where they sat they could hear the message. He never missed an opportunity to promote the gospel.

He took a great interest in Eddie too, and was never too busy to make him simple Indian toys, or to find him insects which doubled as playthings! He made Eddie his first blowgun and provided the seeds for ammunition. He became part of our family, and accompanied us on all our outings.

As Alberto grew up he became even bolder in spreading the gospel. The work was broadening out, and I started to visit Indians in other villages, telling them Bible stories and using a book which had a large picture for each story. Alberto was my usual companion on these trips, and seemed to relate so easily to the people of the other villages—even to one man with whom Biviano was at odds because of an old debt: Luis Benjumea.

Señor Benjumea had foreseen that civilization would eventually come to his village, so he had sent his children away for education long before it reached our remote area of the jungle. I enjoyed Luis's company and our stimulating talks together. Alberto and I visited this village only every other week, however, because gasoline was so scarce—and Luis quickly realized that they were privileged to have us! He made it clear to all the others too.

One day when we visited his family, he called them together for the Bible story, but to his dismay they did not come, even after quite a wait.

"Come now!" he commanded. "Can't you see that Ed Dulka has come to tell us the story, and that he has used his gasoline to get here? This is important!"—just how important he only realized later, when he himself found Christ as Savior.

OUTREACH TO EDUARDO

I often talked with another man, Eduardo Noguera, and in this context and in many others Alberto was invaluable in helping us overcome cultural problems. Eduardo had a real desire to learn about the Bible and would discuss the miracles, the prophecies, and the main characters— but somehow failed to grasp the central truth of salvation by faith in Jesus alone. His Roman Catholic background seemed to make this difficult to accept, no matter how often I pointed it out to him.

Early one morning, Eduardo's daughter came to our house in great distress, asking for medicine for her brother who had been bitten by a poisonous snake. We had no anti-venom, but I quickly gathered the medicines we had used in similar cases. I gave them to the girl, with a note to Eduardo about how to administer them. (I had learned from Alberto that in their culture only one person was allowed to treat a snake bite, and that I would not be able to see the child myself.)

After lunch, Eduardo's daughter returned. "How is your brother?" I asked.

"He is dead," came the reply. My mind reeled. The medicine had worked well in seven other cases. What had gone wrong? What more could I have done? Why had this happened?

"My father wants to know if you have any boards to make a casket," said the girl. Her voice jerked me back to reality.

"I'm sorry," I said, "I haven't. I used the last on my house." It seemed there was no way I could help!

"My father says you may come and visit our house this afternoon. He would like you to bring a camera and take a picture of my brother," she informed me.

As I paddled to Eduardo's village later, I questioned why God had allowed this to happen—trying to understand His purpose in what seemed a backward step.

When I arrived at the village, I was met by some of the people who had become my close friends and who were not ashamed to weep before me. Nearing Eduardo's house, I heard the loud, traditional wailing inside, which subsided as soon as I entered. One by one, the mourners quietly slipped out and I was left alone with Eduardo and the body of his little son, which was lying on a large slab of tree stump in the middle of the small house. The root was covered by the boy's hammock, which was wrapped around his feet and came up to his waist. His hands were folded over his abdomen. Eduardo signaled to me to sit down on one side of the slab and he sat down on the other.

"Did you bring your camera, Ed Dulka?" he asked.

"No," I replied. "I did not want you to remember your son as he is now. I will bring you a picture of him which I took when he was alive and active."

Then Eduardo told me the terrible story. He had poisoned the little stream by their village at the end of the day. He used the juice of a jungle vine called *barbasco*, which takes the oxygen out of the water and causes the fish to come to the surface to breath. Because he had a very severe headache the next morning, he sent his two boys to retrieve the catch. While they were looking for the fish, they passed a hollow tree. The snake was in the tree and struck out at the older boy's thigh with its vicious fangs. He managed to push his brother clear. Then the snake struck again and the older boy fell to the ground screaming. "By the time I got him to the house," said Eduardo, "his leg was swollen and discolored, and he could not speak. When I got your medicine I poured it into his mouth and he stirred and spoke once more. Thank you for helping my son to speak to me one more time. I had my Bible with me, and was asking God to spare my son. His face was full of suffering before he died. Is he suffering now?"

"No," I replied. "He is not suffering now."

"Where is he now?" Eduardo asked.

"He is with God and is happy now. He was very young and had not yet understood God's way of salvation. God is just. You may go to be with him if you believe that Jesus died for your sins and rose again. You and all your family can go to be with God when you die if you put your trust in Jesus." As I told him these things yet again, his eyes lit up with understanding.

"Yes. I know these things now and I will tell them to my family." We sat in silence together, a bond growing between us because of the grief we shared, and because of the hope to come.

"Ed Dulka, will you make a casket for my son?" Eduardo asked.

"Yes, I will—but where can I get the wood?"

"Two of the boys have got an abandoned canoe which drifted down the river. You can have that," he replied.

"I'll bring the casket tomorrow morning," I said, leaving to head home.

Before I had gone two hundred yards, the wailing started up again—but Eduardo's voice rose above it, silencing the mourners. He had something to tell them!

I retrieved the half-rotten canoe, and when I got back home I started right away to make the casket. I lost track of time, thinking of Eduardo and his grieving family. The sun disappeared and I looked up in amazement! Surely it was not nightfall already! I worked frantically to finish the casket and then ran for the house to avoid what seemed to be the onset of a fearful storm. But there was no rainstorm—just this eerie darkness and a rushing wind. The clouds seemed to be centered over the area of Eduardo's village and home.

"That was some wind," said Doreen, as she relit the lamps and served up the evening meal. "It even blew the lamps out. It got dark so quickly, too."

The next morning I was up early, loaded the light casket into the canoe, and paddled to Eduardo's house. Shouldering the casket, I walked towards a group of people which included the man who usually presided over Indian funerals. Word of my arrival reached Eduardo, and he came out, red-eyed, to greet me. A look of understanding passed between us as I turned to go home—wondering how I would feel if my son had been the victim.

That night we had another experience of that curious wind and premature darkness.

A week later I mentioned it to Alberto. "Yes," he said. "We were very frightened."

"But it's not happened before. What caused it?" I pressed.

"We have wind like that when a person dies," he said solemnly—clearly fearful as he recalled the recent events.

"What do you mean?" I asked.

"The old belief is that when a person dies, the devil comes that night in a wind storm. If he causes the candle or lamp to go out, he has claimed the soul of the dead. Eduardo's candle did not go out the day his son died—nor on the following day when he was buried. The devil was unsuccessful."

Alberto's explanations were always so candid and graphic that I shuddered as he finished his account. How Satan had twisted the culture of this people away from the loving God who had created them!

Insights like this from Alberto helped me to know which parts of Biblical doctrine to emphasize and reinforce so that the Indian church would have a solid foundation.

EDDIE SAVES HIS DAD

I had set my fish net out the day

Eduardo's son died. It was ninety feet long and fifteen feet deep. When I returned the following day from delivering the casket, and Eddie had finished his school work, I took him with me to pull in the net. He was taking more responsibility as he grew up. So we climbed into the canoe together, and soon discovered that the net had tangled in the roots of a fallen tree at the bottom of the river during the night, for the swollen water had carried it too far down stream. Eddie and I began pulling in the net, working our way towards the problem area.

It became obvious that I would have to dive down to the riverbed, and I didn't like the thought! (It didn't quite tie up with my earlier schoolboy dreams of being a skin-diver.) The river was fifteen feet deep at this point, and the pressure would hurt my ears. The water was so black and muddy that I would be able to see only a few feet ahead of me—and my lungs would ache for air. It would be a dangerous undertaking.

I adjusted my swimming goggles, told Eddie not to let the rest of the net slip out of the boat, took a deep breath and plunged in—feeling my way along the net. The current was so strong that I was quickly carried beyond the net; then I found myself on the riverbed, located the tangle and began to unwind it. My ears hurt and my lungs were bursting, but I didn't want to make that dive again! "One more try," I urged myself—and suddenly the net was free. I grabbed it and bunched it in my hand, intent only on getting to the surface for air. In my haste I let the net go and it billowed over me, the swift current wrapping it around me. I struggled with the net, desperate to get to the surface. I felt it go over my head and arms . . . then my arms went through it and I reached for the surface. My fingers broke the water and I could see the sun shining on the disrupted surface. So close! Then the net dragged me down again. How could this happen? What would become of my family? What would become of the church? Satan laughed hideously into my mind—"It's over," he crowed gleefully.

I pushed upwards with my last vestige of strength, and my face broke the surface. "Take my hand!" Eddie shouted frantically.

Gulping in air and water, I yelled back, "You take mine!"—before being dragged down again. Then I saw the shadow of the canoe above me, as Eddie negotiated it towards me. Another lunge and my hand broke the surface, but my face did not. Suddenly I felt Eddie's small hand wrap itself around my wrist, pulling my hand towards the canoe and placing my fingers over the sideboard. Still under the water, I knew now that it would be all right. Clinging to the canoe, I at last freed myself from the net and looked at Eddie's terrified little face. "It's all right now, son. Thank you for your help. I could never have managed without you."

Eddie was becoming a young man very early in life. I hauled myself out of the water, and for some time lay on the bottom of the canoe, gulping in air and saying over and over again, "Thank You, Lord." God had strengthened the weak arms of my son and made him the means of my salvation. God would also use us, weak vessels as we were, to bring His salvation to the Carapana Indians.

BACK TO AMERICA

Shortly after the fishing net episode, Doreen and the children took a six-month break in the capital city of Bogotá to await the arrival of our fourth child, Cheryl. We were also beginning to plan our furlough back to the U.S.A., after nearly three years in the jungle.

We had watched with pleasure as a relationship developed between Alberto and Ameria. They were both favorites with our family and with Biviano. Both were Christians, and this meant they would not have to face the dilemma of being married off to an unbelieving partner. We rejoiced that they would set up Christian home. Soon after their marriage, they moved off into Ameria's mother's old house, a four-hour journey away through the jungle. We saw little of Ameria after that, but Alberto came back once a month, usually to attend a church service. Eventually news came through of the birth of their first child, a girl they called Inez.

Our furlough plans were now well under way, and we were looking forward to meeting our families in the U.S.A. and the folks who had so faithfully prayed for us and supported us. We had lived through three-and-a-half tough years, facing hardship, hunger and even death, and the anticipated glamor of a missionary life had certainly been far from reality. But at the same time, we were grateful to God that the beginnings of a church had emerged among the Carapanas.

Alberto and Ameria moved back to Nazareth before we left, and for three days we tried to visit them . . . but Ameria and the baby were always missing. Then one day Amy came home crying. She had seen Inez and she pleaded with Doreen to go and look at the baby's feet. They were all twisted, and Luisa was hurting her by trying to straighten them. Doreen and I went immediately, and Ameria, with both fear and hope on her face, unwrapped the baby's clubfeet, which were at complete right angles to the sides of her legs. Doreen groaned. If the feet were not attended to very soon, Inez would have no hope of survival. It was a miracle she was still alive, for according to local Indian custom Luisa should have buried her deformed grandchild alive at birth. Ameria was sure of God's love for her child, and of our help, and so far had saved Inez from death.

We could sense a new reserve in Alberto. He was not yet mature enough in his faith to realize that we do not always see an immediate answer to the "whys?" of our circumstances. We were leaving for a year's furlough within a few weeks, but we assured Alberto and Ameria that as soon as we got out of the jungle we would see the staff of the Colombian WEC hospital, where Cheryl had been born, and make full arrangements for the baby's care. This we were able to do before we flew on to the U.S.A.

Once we were back in the U.S.A., Colombia seemed like a dream—much of it a bad one! The more we readjusted to the ease and affluence of life back home, the further away the Carapana villages seemed.

Towards the end of our furlough, our thoughts drifted back to those three-and-a-half tough years. Doreen could not bear the thought of going back. I was bound by a sense of duty: we must go. Naturally, we consulted our heavenly Director, and the clear word came to us both, "Go back!" This was something we felt inside of us and knew that only by obeying the command could we enjoy a deep inner peace.

News came from Colombia that the

Communist guerrillas had captured one of the Wycliffe Bible translators. How we fasted and prayed for his release, confident that he would be saved! But the sad news came a month and a half after his capture: Chet Bitterman had been killed by the guerrillas.

We knew now that it was impossible to return! No one would expect us to—least of all our families. But God's word was just the same. "Go back!"

However much we rationalized with God, reminding Him that we would probably be killed too, we could not get around the inescapable fact that He was saying "Go!" It came repeatedly, in spite of all our convincing reasons and arguments.

Obedience to that command took a lot of deep soul-searching, and it was a purifying experience to abandon all the excuses and hesitations which stood between us and total obedience. We were reminded of 2 Corinthians 5:15: "He died for all, that they who live should not henceforth live unto themselves, but unto Him who died for them, and rose again." Jesus had died for us, and by His grace we were alive. Really alive! We belonged to Him, and whatever the cost, we had to go back.

ALBERTO, THE PRODIGAL SON

After a year's furlough we were back in Colombia—all the farewells, formalities and paperwork behind us. From Bogotá Eddie and I flew out to the edge of our jungle parish one day, taking with us some supplies, and Doreen and the girls followed the next day. The airstrip was in a village an hour's journey by motorboat from Nazareth, so Eddie and I borrowed a canoe and paddles, and paddled downriver for three hours to our home. The Indians were quite surprised to see us for they had had no warning of our return.

We arrived at our own dock unobserved, and unloaded all our gear into the house. Then we walked over to Biviano's house to say hello. As we crossed the basketball court that separated our two houses, I could see many, many empty liquor bottles strewn around the village, and noticed a general untidiness that had not been there before. I stepped into Biviano's house and he looked up from his work, but because my back was to the light as I stood in the doorway he didn't recognize me. Then I greeted him in his own language, and with a shout the family rushed to welcome us!

They could not believe that we had arrived undetected! We exchanged stories throughout the afternoon about what had happened to us all during the past year. When evening began to fall, Eddie and I excused ourselves and went back to our house to unpack lamps and bedding from our storeroom.

The next day we tried frantically to make the place habitable, to be ready for Doreen and the girls. Many sections of the building had been eaten through by termites or had just rotted away during our absence. It would take major repairs to get the house back in order.

When Doreen and the girls arrived they had the grace to compliment us on doing a good job, but it took all of us two weeks' hard work before the house was really in order.

We held no church services while we were getting the house ready and readjusting to jungle life, but we were very conscious that there was a strangely subdued atmosphere in the village. Something was being hidden from us. I had tried to get help with repairs to our roof, but had been told that everyone was too busy, and it gradually became evident that all the men were fully involved in the growing of coca leaves for the making of cocaine. We were sick at heart to see the choice they had made while we were away.

It was good to see Alberto and Ameria again. They had built a house right outside our back door, and what a blessing it was to see little Inez running about and playing with the other children. The white scars on her ankles were the only evidence that she had ever been different from them.

After I had been back about two weeks, I went over one afternoon to talk to Biviano.

"We have been very busy with our housecleaning, but now things are all ready," I started out.

"Yes. That is good. I am sure many insects moved in while you were away," he replied.

"They nearly ate the whole house!" I exclaimed. "But now that it is ready, we wondered if you wanted to start church services again."

Biviano was silent for several moments, then said very resignedly, "Well, I guess that is the reason you are living here again. If that is why you have come back, we will have to start services again."

It was obvious that a real conflict was going on inside him, and equally obvious that none of the villagers had been living a Christian life for some time. Even though they read their Bibles and listened to Christian radio programs, their lives and occupation denied the gospel. So we set up a modified version of our former pattern, holding services on Monday, Wednesday and Friday evenings and on Sunday mornings.

By this time people from other villages were visiting us, some to welcome us back but most to see if we had items to trade. With their new wealth from the cocaine business they had money to burn. I had warned them many times before going on furlough not to get involved in the cocaine traffic, but the immense riches of the business eventually had drawn each one in.

Their own use of the drug was very limited—comparable perhaps to three or four aspirins or a cup of strong coffee. They would chew coca leaves to combat pain, or hunger, and to keep them awake when they hunted or fished throughout the night. They had no comprehension at all of the ultimate use of cocaine once the leaves had been bought from them. They knew only that it was a quick and easy way to make money.

We had been contemplating running a village store, so that the people could trade for things they needed—but it soon became evident that they had all they needed! While I was still wondering about the store, a boat arrived at Nazareth. It was a coca-leaf buyer's boat. Thirty-five feet long and a little over a yard wide, it was packed with every imaginable type of trade goods, including things that we ourselves could never afford. We watched in astonishment as the people from our village went down to the boat and took everything their hearts desired! No money changed hands. It was all done on credit. In two weeks' time the cocainer would be back to collect his payment in coca leaves.

The idea of running a store was useless! We could never compete with the cocaine dealer. The idea had been to get in touch with more people, in order to share the gospel with them. How would we do it now?

There was still the feeling that more was being hidden from us, and very few people came to see us. It was apparent that in surrounding villages there was a lot of drinking and drunkenness, and I was puzzled to know why it hadn't reached Nazareth—especially as I'd seen all those empty bottles. The folks in our village would even report on who had traveled out to buy liquor, how much they had brought back, and which village was currently drunk.

While we were still waiting for more contact with the local Carapanas, some of the cocaine traffickers came back. They made crude shelters at the back of Nazareth—just pieces of plastic draped over poles. I gradually got to know each of the cocainers, and tried to share the gospel with them. The first to set up trade at the back of Nazareth was a man I'd known years before. He had been in one business after another, taking on a new one when the old one became unprofitable.

This cocainer was a small man, but he carried a large .45 caliber pistol. I gave this weapon a disapproving look when I first saw it, and after that he never carried it openly in Nazareth. An Indian boy was working for him, and I recognized him as coming from a Christian village where I had once attended a conference. As I left the cocaine camp, I called to the boy and told him our service was at 7 P.M. and that he and anyone else would be welcome. The whole crew came that night, and on many subsequent occasions. They were very impressed, having never heard the gospel before. One night, as they left the service I heard them call out to Alberto, "Good night, Loco." I was shocked! Surely they could not mean that? Alberto was fun-loving, but certainly not crazy! But as the days went by, we realized that *Loco* was a generally accepted nickname for Alberto, and one which puzzled us very much.

The more we saw of the cocainers' popularity and the way the local people flocked to them, the more we realized our need of some new way to bring the villagers within hearing of the gospel. We had been back five months, and it was now Christmas. We were sure that if we held a Christmas party, all the people of the Caño Ti would come. We had had these parties before, and they lasted three days. This time the people came willingly enough, but their interest was short lived.

Soon after Christmas, Ameria's brother brought liquor to the village. Everyone got drunk, and then there was bickering and fighting. Shotguns went off during the night. The self-imposed "stopper" which had kept the villagers in check since our return had now blown out! They were drunk for three whole days. Once the stopper was out, there was no controlling them, and every weekend became a drunken party.

Now we began to see Ameria go into a shell, and to realize why Alberto had earned his nickname. When he was in one of his drunken rages she was afraid to come to our services or to do anything that would annoy Alberto. He surely did become a madman! He also made an open break with us, staying away from the services and forbidding his children to play with ours. Every weekend the whole crowd would indulge in drunken orgies in Nazareth—or travel to another village and cause havoc there. Many times we had a service with only our own family: the Indians were too drunk to attend. They also neglected their gardens, and their children frequently went hungry.

One day an accident occurred which we hoped would bring our villagers to their senses. While they were making a garden (all the time in a drunken stupor), a tree was cut too deeply, fell in the wind, and a branch as thick as a man's body broke off—hitting a man on the head and killing him instantly. I helped to bring him out of the jungle back to Nazareth, made the casket, and dug the grave. We buried him the same evening. We had a service that night and talked of Heaven, Hell, and the uncertainty of life. Many listened who had not been at all open before.

When we were alone together, I asked Biviano if he had ever shared the gospel with the man who had died. Biviano said he had talked to the man, but he had never become a Christian. From Biviano's reactions I thought that he might now have had enough of his present careless life-style, but I was wrong.

It hurt us to see these people among whom we had lived and worked being so sadly deceived. We knew they were in inner turmoil and conflict, but they seemed to go from bad to worse, especially after they started not only drinking liquor but smoking a by-product of cocaine which fogged their minds and made them depraved.

One night I finished teaching and turned to Biviano, who normally translated for the women present. He was looking at the floor and then said, with a great effort, "I don't know how to preach anymore." A few nights later I had an opportunity to speak to him alone.

"Biviano . . . why did you stop the services when we left?"

"We carried on at first," he said, "but gradually the people lost interest and stopped coming. Finally only my son Luis and I were left, and the others would come and mock us." Biviano's tone was full of remorse, knowing that the decision to abandon the services had brought all this present trouble on them.

Many of the new people who had moved into Nazareth while we'd been away were Ameria's relatives, and two of her brothers were unreliable and shiftless. They had a great influence on Alberto, who defied his father Biviano in order to go along with them. In drunken brawls he would always take their side against Biviano. Then for some unaccountable reason, Alberto stopped drinking and joined the cocainers in their traffic. Just as he'd been an information man for us when he was younger, he now became indispensable to the cocainers.

Now that he was sober, Alberto became a good friend and neighbor again and we did many things together. But although we depended on each other as neighbors, he always withdrew when the gospel was mentioned. The inner battle he was fighting made him frustrated, and when I was not around he would take his frustration out on anyone near him—especially our children.

In spite of his waywardness and harsh behavior we loved Alberto and kept close to him for Ameria's sake. She bore the brunt of his outburts—usually verbal abuse in Indian style, but sometimes physical abuse too.

Those first two years of our ministry in the second term were very hard. No one wanted us or our message. We had many church services with only one or two Indians—some with only our own family.

"God," I cried, "we have preached Your Word and lived among these people—but they are rejecting You! Isn't it time for us to shake the dust off our feet and move on somewhere else?"

God's still, small voice came back: "Stay." He had His plans for the Carapana Indians.

We had to learn obedience once more, even though we could not see how God would ever change these people.

COME TOGETHER

Within the first year after furlough, we knew we had to build a new house. Ed had patched and replaced many beams, walls and pieces of bark flooring, but the termites and roaches had won. Ed asked at every village if anyone wanted to work for pay in helping him gather poles for the new house. But no one wanted to do hard labor when they could make more picking coca leaves. This led to a three-year job for Ed, who had to do all the building himself in his spare time from the ministry.

We decided to build a two-story house, as it would take less roofing and give us more privacy. Amy was becoming a young lady and was asking for her own bedroom. Since we could get no help in gathering and cutting palm leaves for a thatched roof, we decided we would buy zinc sheets in Mitú and bring them up river by canoe. This would save Ed a lot of work and also give us clean rain water for drinking. Never having to boil drinking water again nor having to haul buckets of water from the river for household uses would be fantastic!

Slowly the new house began to take shape, with four bedroom upstairs and the kitchen and living room downstairs. An enclosed stairway divided the ground-floor area.

Our ministry certainly went through a dry spell, but we continued to make lasting friendships. Ameria was no longer free to spend time with me, but God gave me a new companion, Beti. This was a totally foreign name in that culture, and we never discovered how she had acquired it. She was a young, single woman from Puerto Guavina, the next village upriver from Nazareth. Beti spoke Spanish more fluently than any of the Caño Ti women, and that enabled me to have much more meaningful conversations with her.

We tried many ways of reaching the local women. The Indian girls were eager to have some new-style dresses such as they had seen elsewhere, so Beti and I put our heads together and decided to start a sewing class. I showed them my method of cutting out a garment using a paper pattern, but that completely mystified them! They could not see the connection between the paper and the dress. Their method was much simpler. They would look hard and long at the person to be "fitted"—and then cut away at the material. When it seemed to be the right size and shape, they would try it against their "model," and I was amazed at their accuracy! After many attempts to sew together, we had to abandon that project because we could not learn each other's methods. The Indian girls explained that my way was work, whereas theirs was relaxation. They continued to come to me for needles, thread, and other accessories, however— and we always showed off our creations to each other.

One day the nearby government schoolteacher asked for ten men and ten women to represent the Caño Ti area by taking a trip to a model village on another river. The village had received a lot of help from the government to set it up and make it prosperous. The government wanted other Indians to see it, and then they would be given help in copying the pattern of that model village. The journey there involved a day's paddle up the Caño Ti, a four-hour overland walk, and a further day's paddle down the other river.

Beti and her brother were two of the twenty asked to represent the Caño Ti Indians, and when they returned from seeing the model village they could talk of nothing else. They told us how organized it was, about the neat houses with their zinc roofs, and about the prosperity the people enjoyed. All the representatives were young people, and they were full of enthusiastic ideas for making life better in the Caño Ti. They wanted to change everything!

The older people had already lived through too many dramatic changes and were out of their element already. They were still in charge, and were not ready for all these bright ideas. We tried to mediate, and to explain to the young people that the changes that had been achieved in the model village had taken years—not months.

Not long after this event, we seized the ideal opportunity to invite more local people to another village—this time a Christian one—for a conference. It was to be held in a Christian Cubéo village, and there would be a week's teaching in the Christian faith, and fellowship with mature Indian believers. We would meet with our Colombian co-workers, the Ortiz family. Leonel and Belgica Ortiz and their three daughters were Colombians from Cali, and had received a call from God to work among the Cubéo Indians in the Vaupés Province. They had been working now as Christian schoolteachers in a neighboring Cubéo tribe, but we lived so far apart that fellowship was possible only at this annual conference. At other times we kept in touch by sending letters with Indians going in their direction.

For months we encouraged our faltering Christians and any others who showed interest to go with us to the conference, but they all had some excuse and separately refused. I was thankful that Beti had promised to attend, even though in this man's world she would not get much of a hearing when she got back. She was very eager to compare this Christian village with the model village she had seen. The Christian village was called Sabana (Spanish for "Savannah"). It was located on an extensive plain of sandstone rock, and was composed of five families who wanted to live for Christ and to stay free of the cocaine traffic. Beti's father agreed to her going as long as she was with us.

On Sunday, the day before we left, Ed called everyone together for the service, and when it was over we had a meal and saw to last minute preparations. Ed and I were both looking forward to companionship and fellowship with Leonel and Belgica; we missed this kind of interaction so much. We also looked forward to being with the fine Sabana Christians.

People were in and out of the house as we packed, and Beti assured us that she would be on time the next morning.

At the end of the day, packing finished, we gathered around the kerosene lamp for our youth meeting—made up of our own four children! We sang, had a lesson, sang again—and then got to bed early to be ready for the next day's trip.

We were up at dawn and began loading the canoe right after breakfast and morning prayers. It promised to be a lovely day, and not too hot for the six-hour river journey. Some of the men who had brought Beti down from her village stayed around to watch the packing, and as Ed was making a trip down the steps with baggage, Biviano appeared. He watched Ed load the cargo, and nodded approvingly.

When Ed made his way back up the steps, Biviano spoke to him. "Since there are no men to represent the Christians of the Caño Ti, I will go myself."

Joy burst within Ed! This was the answer to so many prayers that God would do something new among these people!

"That will be fine," said Ed. "Go and pack quickly"—keeping his face as impassive as the Indian's.

We knew what it had cost Biviano to make that decision, and that he was no doubt motivated purely by his love for Ed. But we also knew that he would not be disappointed.

When others in the village realized that Biviano was going, four teenagers decided to take advantage of the trip too. We took all who would go, realizing the importance of having young men trained to be leaders in the church. By 8:30 A.M. we were off—with six Indians and six Dulkas on board.

By noon we had reached Mandí, the site of the treacherous rapids. We had not been that way for over a year, but as we greeted the people we were aware of the new "anti-foreigner" feeling that was becoming increasingly common in villages where our Christian ministry was not known. There was a new, large school here and we found that the teachers were "anti-foreigner" in sentiment too.

Most of us got out of the canoe above the rapids; then Biviano and Ed took it safely through. Once the canoe was docked at the lower side of the rapids, we took out the picnic lunch and enjoyed the break—lazing in the warm sunshine. Our bodies had been cramped and were boat-weary, so it was refreshing to keep changing our position and just watch the swirling water go by. But we could not afford to delay too long! Soon the bowls were washed and repacked, everything and everybody back in the boat, and we were on our way downriver again.

Within an hour we entered the river

on which the village of Sabana lay, but I couldn't recognize the landmarks, and the journey seemed longer than I had remembered. Then about 2:30 P.M., Biviano's right arm shot out and directed Ed to a little creek. We had arrived!

We were warmly greeted by our Sabana friends, though the six Caño Ti Indians were very shy and reticent. After the preliminary greetings, and being offered refreshing drinks, the Sabana folks showed us the rooms we would occupy and helped us unload our baggage. With that chore done, the men of the village returned to their job of preparing the chapel for the meetings.

Ed helped to set up the hammocks and ropes, and the tarpaulins to keep the wind out. (The idea of having solid walls to hide behind never entered our heads anymore.) He then put up a makeshift table for me outside the house, near where our cooking would be done, and went to gather firewood.

Later Ed joked with the men as they worked on the chapel, and bombarded them with questions about what they had been doing since we last met. He also spent time with Eddie, helping him set his fishhooks, while the girls and I went to look at the local "bath tub"—a large pool below the cascading waterfall. We decided which paths would be most easily traveled, and where we would designate the toilet area. About 4:30 we were forced into our house by a rainstorm.

The village chief had taken the Caño Ti Indians to another house. They did not like this much, but knew better than to argue against Indian protocol: the chief assigns your living quarters. We learned that we would be sharing our 15-by-15-foot room with the Ortiz family and their house helper, so we rearranged our hammocks to make room for another six! This is done by hanging one hammock directly above another.

By 5:15 the rain had stopped, and we heard the noise of an approaching motorboat. The Ortiz family had arrived—thoroughly soaked and cold. We helped carry their belongings to the house, and I ran ahead to make hot chocolate and coffee. Seeing Belgica brought back memories of *our* earlier days in the jungle, and how hopelessly difficult and unfamiliar everything had been then.

Once the children were in their hammocks, Leonel went off to see the villagers, to try to organize a schedule for these few precious days together. We endeavored to show a film that night, only to discover that the generator Leonel had hauled all that way was inoperable! The day was done, and we were all exhausted. Tomorrow would be a new day.

There was a large, flat, sandstone rock some fifty yards from the house, and the four of us ended the day there relaxing in prayer and fellowship together—sharing the blessings and problems of the past year, and drinking in the peace and beauty of the moonlit tropical night around us. Then we outlined a program for the next day, discussed goals for the teaching sessions, and voiced personal prayer requests. At last, reluctantly, we said good-night.

After breakfast the next morning, Leonel and Ed shared the program with the Sabana Indian leaders. Once it had been modified to their satisfaction, the schedule was accepted—with Ed leading teaching sessions from 8 to 10 A.M. and Leonel from 10:30 to 12 noon. We all ate together at noon, each family contributing to the meal. Then we had an extended break, during which we bathed, had family time, chatted with friends, and hiked over the beautiful terrain around us. Around 6 P.M. everyone joined together again for a service with one of the Indian laymen sharing. As the day ended, we looked forward to returning to our rock for that precious time of praise and fellowship; and we have since often looked back on those wonderful moments in that beautiful setting.

Beti, Biviano, and the young folks

were happy in their accommodations, but whenever there was a break in proceedings Beti herded the teenagers over to our place to make sure they got in on the treat of the day. She also enjoyed getting to know the woman of the house where she was staying. Only during the previous year had she become a Christian. Beti told us that the woman's husband would sit by the fire with her every evening and go over all of that day's teaching, and that every morning they would read the Bible and pray together. Beti was really delighted by the way these Sabana Christians accepted her as one of themselves. Usually Indians do not readily accept others whom they do not know, but Beti saw the difference in these Christians.

Biviano spent a lot of his time with the older Indians, discussing many aspects of things which came to his mind, and absorbing all the teaching at the conference. He and Ed discussed practical issues too—comparing Sabana with Nazareth, including looking at the two hogs the Sabana Christians were raising and wondering if it would be a feasible project back in Nazareth. They talked about possible food supplies for the animals, and how they could market some of the hogs for profit as well as using some to feed the villagers.

Ed and I took a few hikes with our

family, collecting orchids which were quite different from those in the Caño Ti area. We also had lovely, memorable outings with the Ortiz family—up a beautiful creek and past a series of waterfalls and pools. The days went too quickly. Our relationship with Leonel and Belgica deepened and we became like one family.

On the final day of the conference, some of the Sabana leaders came and asked if the next conference could be held in the valley of the Caño Ti. Oh how we loved that idea, but the decision was not ours to make.

"You must ask Biviano," said Ed. "He runs our village, and only he can give the invitation."

Ed went off to let Biviano know about the request, while Belgica and I discussed possibilities of getting together again. Easter, nine months away, seemed the only opportunity. During the closing meeting Biviano was asked publicly about hosting the conference at Easter. He stood to his feet. He had changed during the conference and had rededicated his life to the Lord. He chose his words carefully, replying that he felt there was inadequate accommodation at Nazareth, and no chapel. The leaders discussed his answer among themselves, then said that the accommodation was not the main issue. The most important thing was to strengthen the

Caño Ti Christians, as well as help evangelize the area. Biviano agreed to host the meetings!

We all knew what a big responsibility this decision would put on us if things were to be ready for the following year's conference. For Biviano it was a difficult step. He had walked with the Lord for many years and had become strong in his faith, preaching and teaching others. Then the great temptation of material gain through the cocaine trade had caused him to stumble. He had eventually become so involved in the wickedness that went with the trade that he had found it hard to come back to God and ask for forgiveness. Now that he had, he knew he would face a lot of ridicule back in the Caño Ti. We knew, however, that God was going to make him a light among the Carapanas!

Beti shared with me that before she went to the conference she had thought she knew what it was to be a Christian. After living with an Indian family who put their faith into practice, she too desired to live a true Christian life. When we got back home, she was bursting to tell her family what she had learned. The government's model village had nothing to compare with the things she had experienced at Sabana.

PICK UP THE PIECES

Within a week of our return from conference, the weekend drunken orgies in our village came to an end. Biviano and his oldest son Luis also gave up their coca fields and refused to do any more trade with the cocainers.

The attendance at Sunday church services rose to between twenty and thirty—a source of great encouragement, and a cause for some real hard work! Our village had to host the congregation for dinner every Sunday after church, and our prowess as hunters and fishermen was tested every Saturday in order to provide enough food. Even in this we Christians had a testimony, because God always provided enough not only for us attenders but for the *rest* of the villagers in Nazareth, who *shared* our catch!

Our week-night meetings were changed to Tuesday and Thursday, and

Tuesday became very special to us as Christians. We departed from the usual Bible teaching routine and gave the entire evening to prayer—the value of which we were trying to teach our converts by practice. They learned how to pray and could be called on to do so at any time. Biviano added a real dimension of urgency to these times. He might occasionally miss another service for some valid reason, but he would never miss a prayer time; it was a life-or-death matter to him. There were usually four of us: Biviano, Luis, Doreen and myself—and we were often joined by Biviano's wife, Emilia, and our own daughter, Amy, now twelve. Sometimes others from the village joined us too.

Our pattern was to start with a song, then discuss news for prayer and relate answers to former prayers. We then started in earnest with the current prayer targets: the leaders of the neighboring villages, and the people of our own village—mentioning them by name. We know that God heard, but so did everyone outside! The "windows" of our house were merely holes in the bark walls, and the walls themselves were so thin that people in all the other houses could hear us. This added another dimension to our prayers! The "targets" knew they were being prayed for. Biviano always led these sessions, and then the rest of us would follow in prayer—first the men and then the women, led by Emilia. These times really enriched our lives and fellowship, and prepared the ground for what God would do at Easter.

NEW PROVISIONS

During the time the villagers in Nazareth had grown coca leaves their vegetable gardens had deteriorated, so when they stopped producing cocaine they had no food reserves to fall back on. All that year after Biviano took the lead in abandoning the cocaine trade, such food in Nazareth was very scarce. Hence Biviano had to plan a lot of work for the village, to restore supplies and aim towards a better economy. Luis was also busy building his own house. Our goal as a little group of believers was to have a church building ready for the Easter conference—but where would the time and money come from?

We got together as a village and decided to fell trees, make a raft with the logs, and take them to Mitú to sell. I took part in the discussions but could only work part-time on the actual project as I was teaching Eddie in fifth grade and Amy in sixth grade for the school year.

Biviano and Luis went out every day for two weeks, marking the trees that would supply suitable wood. The village food supply rose sharply once the men began to work on the trees in the jungle. The more time they spent there, the more seeds, nuts—and sometimes meat—they brought home.

I spent every Saturday working with them, leaving the actual tree cutting to Biviano and Luis. I marked the trees into eleven-foot sections and chopped them through. We produced thirty-two logs the first Saturday, and at that stage they seemed not too far from the water's edge. I joined the men in searching for jungle food too—and I acquired a lot of knowledge of the area, as well as bags of edible seeds for the family.

On the second Saturday when I went to work, all the trees had been sectioned. There were seven men on the job, and we had to roll all the logs to the river to make the raft. The "not too far from the water's edge" now seemed like five-hundred yards instead of a hundred! We had to carve out twelve-foot-wide paths from the piles of logs to the river; then two of us, each with a pole, would push a single log along the path. Each thrust of the pole moved the log two or three feet, and where the path came to a tree which was too big to be felled, we had to negotiate the log around it. It also had to be maneuvered around curves in the path, and over a makeshift bridge to the depository in the river. The seven of us pushed forty logs to the water that Saturday, then left this strenuous activity to catch up on other jobs which meanwhile had been neglected in the village.

Many evenings were spent in talking over the price of logs, reckoning how much we would get and how the money would be spent. A large portion would be needed to buy gasoline so that we could go further up river to gather the right kind of leaves for the church roof. The remainder would go to buy essential supplies for the villagers—batteries, lead ammunition, gunpowder and fishhooks.

Biviano and Luis spent three days collecting vines with which to tie the logs together. After teaching school one day, I had a quick lunch and then paddled excitedly down the river to help the two men, and to learn more about making a raft. I found a raft securely tied to some branches along the river, but Biviano and Luis were nowhere in sight. I ducked in and out of the brush along the river, looking for a trail so that I could follow them. Then I heard the sound of a canoe being paddled. I waited for its arrival. Luis came into sight with his canoe very low in the water—a green log having been tied under the canoe. Luis greeted me and grinned at the expression on my face, at the same time pointing me to the trail I had not found.

I met Biviano just as he was pushing off with his canoe and a similar log undercarriage. He greeted me too, and pointed to more logs at the bottom of the creek! Those green ones just would not float. I got out of my canoe, rescued a log from under the water, and strapped it under my canoe with a vine. Dripping wet, I climbed back into the canoe and followed the trail out to the raft. It was hard going, but we made trip after trip until all the logs in that area were at the raft. I watched, fascinated, at the expertise of Biviano and Luis as they tied the logs in place. I knew a little of the art—but not enough. The strength and safety of the whole raft depended on how well the logs were tied together.

Finally, when the raft was completed, all the men gave their time to hunting, fishing, and gathering food for the journey. Some of the food was for the travelers, the rest was to sell in Mitú. The raft was made up of 105 logs, and was supposed to have a lean-to roof to shelter the travelers, but when it took off on its journey it was still bare. It would be a three-day journey, exposed to all the elements—not an exciting prospect. The thought of the Mandí rapids was even more frightening. A raft had been shattered there earlier in the year, driven by the fearsome current. But God's protecting hand was on our villagers. Biviano and Luis handled the raft expertly through the rapids and reached Mitú unharmed, where the logs were sold.

THE NAZARETH CHURCH IS BUILT

Our anticipation of the Easter conference grew as we saw one goal after another accomplished. The next project on the list was to collect the leaves for the church roof. The men had gone upriver for four days to do this, and in their absence I had the job of catching and supplying fish for the rest of the village! On the afternoon of the fourth day we heard the sound of a motor—far up the river. The plan had been to use paddles to bring the leaves down the river, so we feared that something had gone wrong.

A loaded boat came into view. The motorman had to stand to see out. It was Luis—peering out from a pile of leaves! He greeted us, and after he'd had a meal he explained where the rest of the men were, and why he was alone. The river had not co-operated with them: the water had been too low to use the larger boat and bring all the leaves. After an hour's rest Luis came out of his house and together we unloaded the leaves. He had also brought a catch of fish to help with our food supplies. The following morning he was off again, promising to return in three days.

Those were days which Biviano cherished, because Alberto had gone on the trip to help with the leaves for the church. It was a long time since he had shown any interest at all, and he had been one of Biviano's prime targets in those Tuesday prayer meetings! Biviano's remorse at having led his family into harmful ways was now matched by his prayerful interest in Alberto and Ameria, and his efforts to get them away from the influence of Ameria's family and under his own. None of Ameria's folks would have anything to do with the gospel, but Alberto was slowly coming back, and his help with the church project made Doreen and me very excited.

The work party eventually returned— tired, grimy and grinning—almost submerged beneath leaves. After they'd had a quick bite to eat, we began hauling the bundles of leaves up the bank. Each bundle weighed 100 pounds—but we were all in high spirits as we unloaded them. This completed another goal for the coming conference.

Living with these Indians gave us a new concept of time. It was no use trying to hurry them, or worrying about their easy-going manner. Every event in their world had it's proper season—and when it came, everything else was put aside, no matter how important. Now the church-building work was put aside, because it was time to start to cut and plant gardens for the next crop. Weeks would be spent on this, and it must be done properly. The future food supply depended on it.

The next event was Christmas, and we set aside a week for celebrations. There was a lot of cleaning in the village beforehand, and a great gathering in of food. It was one of our favorite times of the year, and we had our usual three-day party, with nearly all the villages joining us. Each person received some little gift—and each one heard the gospel. While they were all in a mood of celebration and enjoyment, we told them all about the Easter conference, and invited them to come to that celebration too.

A month before Easter the gardens were in order, the walls of Luis's house had been finished—and Biviano indicated that it was now time to finish the church building! We knew it could never be done in a month, but God had been talking to Doreen and me about a possible solution. We had completely moved into the new house and no longer needed the old one, except for one room which we used as our children's schoolroom. I suggested to Biviano one Tuesday evening that we should dismantle the part of the old house we didn't need and add the materials from that on to the existing meeting room to form the new church. The suggestion was considered for a few days and then approved. However, it was far more complicated than I had expected! Their idea of expanding the meeting room was not to move a wall out but to do a complete renovation.

The Monday we started was more like a party day than a workday. Everyone turned out to see what would be uncovered when the old roof, floor and walls came down. Biviano had in his mind exactly how each piece would be reused. The walls came down first, and were piled neatly on one side. Then the pieces of palm bark were lifted from the floor and piled separately. This caused great amusement, for underneath the "floor" were all sorts of items which we hadn't seen for many years—cutlery, tools, toys, etc. After that there was a small-scale archeological dig, as folks sifted the sand for other items. We retrieved a can opener and a drill bit that were valueless to the Indians, and let them carry off the rest as trophies. Those items brought back some early memories!

Soon everything that could be discovered had been discovered, and eventually the framework of the floor was taken out and the area was swept clean of debris, which was then burned. The following day the Indians were busy making scaffolding under the roof, and after dinner the roof was taken down section by section. Then most of the supporting poles came down, leaving only six to be used in the new building. The rest of the week was spent in gathering new poles, and in routine work around the village.

On Monday everyone turned out to help, including the women. Each of the structure poles was selected by Biviano before being put into its proper position. The pride that he was taking in the building was unimaginable! It meant more to him—and to us—than just a church building! More and more were attending our services, and folks around were watching to see what would happen now that the village had come back to Christ. Biviano was glad about the renewed interest and felt sure that the building would be a symbol to draw those who showed concern. To others it would be a reminder of God—in the only Christian village in the area.

After the poles were up I was called upon to put the roof back—because I was taller than all the others! The old roof went back on, but the sections were placed close together to cover the holes. Then the new leaves were used to finish the remainder of the roof. The building had been widened by two feet. The walls went up quickly—using the old walls and the bark from the floor.

A few mornings later we were disturbed in our school work by a constant thumping next door. We peered through a crack in the wall and saw Biviano, Luis and Alberto beating the dirt floor to make it hard. They each had a log, with holes drilled through the top for a pole handle— and the contraptions worked like sledge hammers, but covered more ground. The pounding went on all day and part of the following one, the floor being sprinkled with water between the onslaughts. Their method made a very good, firm surface.

Things now looked shipshape, but Alberto had one more idea for a finishing touch. He came to our house for the materials, and went off to put a coat of white paint on the wall which faced the village. Everyone was proud of the place, and when it was finished it was hard to find seats for all who came.

All that remained now was to make more benches, gather food, and send out invitations to the conference. Our days were filled with activity, but it was a happy time as Doreen and I prepared for the blessing we were sure God would send. Soon a living, witnessing church among the Carapanas would become a reality.

A CHURCH IS BORN

Easter had finally arrived! That long-prayed-for and long-awaited time when, we believed, God would bring many of the Caño Ti Indians to Himself. The fever of preparations was contagious and everyone was talking about the conference.

Biviano and I spent time together sharing our personal expectations and outlining the plans and procedures for the conference. We had promised to show films of the life of Christ, and had invited Wycliffe Bible translators from two different tribes to join us—along with some of the Indians among whom they worked. The Ortiz family was due to arrive the day before the conference started, and the Wycliffe contingent the following morning. Excitement was mounting, and we were full of anticipation of what God would do.

Inevitably, Satan stirred up opposition and caused problems. The good relationship we had enjoyed for three years with the nearby Roman Catholics was disturbed because all the Indians, including those from R.C. villages, were keen to attend the conference. The R.C. church leaders did not understand precisely what the conference was about, so they made a trip through the whole area, forbidding their people to come.

For the first time there were also rumors of guerrilla activity in our particular area. We knew there was a large guerrilla camp about forty miles upriver from Nazareth, but we were separated from it by large, powerful rapids known as the Devil's Cataract. No one could cross that barrier without being noticed, and in any case there was nothing in our area to interest guerrillas. The Wycliffe translators had intercepted information about movements of the guerrillas, and the Indians confirmed this, but the incidents reported were a hundred miles away. It was all too far away to cause us any anxiety.

Late on Tuesday afternoon we heard a motor coming upstream and we lined the banks of the river to see who was arriving. It was Leonel and his party. Sadly Belgica and their younger children could not come because Belgica had tonsilitis, so Leonel had brought only their daughter Bolena. We welcomed them and Henrique, an Indian we had met at

Sabana. Then we were introduced to Placido, a striking Cubéo man, and to Daniel, a student who had been Leonel's motorman for the trip. Eventually the guests were introduced to the whole village. They had heard so much about Leonel and were happy to meet him themselves.

After supper we showed off our village to the visitors, and then got together to discuss the week's teaching plans. I realized that Placido had a real gift for teaching, so I bowed out of that area and gave him my assigned time. Henrique, who had spent time with Biviano at the Sabana conference, drifted over to Biviano's house and spent a long time catching up on all his news. Biviano had lived near Sabana originally, and had been converted there fifteen years earlier—so they knew many of the same people, and their conversation flowed back and forth for some time. Doreen and I were busy hearing all Leonel's news, and learning about the spread of the gospel where he worked—some 150-miles journey from us by river. Then we had one of our precious times of prayer together, focusing on the coming teaching sessions.

The first one was a disappointing anticlimax! When we met for the opening session the next morning only people from our village were present, and even one of our own families from the village had decided to go off visiting friends that day! No one else had arrived since Leonel and his party, and only eight of our Indians were present when we started. Leonel was obviously surprised to see so few, and Biviano was desperately disappointed. I was both surprised and disappointed, but thankful that those eight had turned up, and we were soon all engrossed in the ministry. Leonel taught throughout the morning in Spanish, while Placido translated the message into Cubéo, which most of our Carapana Indians understood. For those who knew neither Spanish nor Cubéo, it was then translated into Carapana or Barasano, another Indian dialect. It was all very time-consuming, but Leonel was thrilled to know that everyone there was receiving the gospel message.

By midafternoon, the Wycliffe workers arrived: Ron Metzger from our local tribe, Bev Brandrup who was translating in the Siriano language, and Linda Criswell, Bev's companion. Three Barasano Indians who had been flown in for the conference came with them. They had all been soaked during a rain shower while they were traveling, so Doreen took the women off for a hot drink while the men unloaded the boat.

Ron had stopped at each village they

had passed on the river, telling the folks that the films had arrived and inviting them to the conference to see one that evening. After supper we started to get ready to show the film. The weather was co-operative, so we hung up a double-bed sheet for a screen, and all the church and house benches were brought out to seat the rapidly growing crowd. People from other villages started arriving at 4:30 P.M., and when it was time for the film, eighty had gathered!

Biviano viewed the large crowd with great satisfaction, and the majority settled down to see their first film ever. It was exceptionally well produced and the people loved it. The sound was in Spanish, so there was a good deal of whispering back and forth in the different Indian languages to make sure everyone knew what was being said. There were three films in the series, and this first one finished at eight o'clock.

Ron headed off for a tiring journey home in the dark. Bev and Linda were ready for bed after their long day. The impact of the film had been great, and the graphic portrayal of the life and betrayal of Jesus had left the Indians with a great deal to think about and discuss in their own villages. Leonel, Doreen and I had our prayer time together, and by the time we had finished, most of our own village was asleep.

Thursday morning showed a sharp increase in attendance, and even more Indians arrived throughout the morning.

"You are like a boat afloat on a great river," Leonel told them, pointing to his drawing. "The river winds this way and that, and in the end it goes over a big waterfall where all is destroyed." His pointer moved over the graphic illustration. "Here is a little creek, narrow and straight. It is different from the great river. If you enter it, you will be on your way to Heaven. You may enter free of charge, but it will cost a lot. Your boat has a motor on it, but on the river you are just drifting with the current. To get out of the grip of the current you must use your motor to enter the little creek: it is too hard to paddle. Your boat must also be loaded with the right things for the journey. Your tank must be filled with gasoline. Have you got all the right things? Is your tank filled with gas, to get you out of the grasp of the big river and into the creek? Or are you going to continue drifting downriver unprepared—heading for the great waterfall?"

Leonel paused, then asked in a serious voice: "Is *your* tank full? Have *you* got Jesus with you? Only He has the power to get you out of the large river that ends in destruction and into the safety of the creek that leads to God."

The river is their life. They readily understood the parallels, and Leonel knew he had made the gospel plain to them.

Placido took the next session, giving his testimony which was very relevant to other young men in the congregation.

"I was born in a Christian village and learned the religion of my father. I went to a Catholic school and received a good education. Then a missionary lady paid for me to go to a Bible Institute, so I could come back to the Vaupés, to teach others. But when I got back, everyone was growing coca and making a lot of money. I decided I would get rich too. My father's religion told me I should not do this—but I had no control over my desires and ambitions. Soon I was entangled in the same snares which I used to condemn in others. I smoked cocaine, I chased women, and I taunted the few older men who tried to have church services and witness to me.

"One day, while brother Leonel was preaching, I walked right into the middle of church. I was very drunk and I shook my finger in his face, telling him that in two years we would drive all the Christians out of the Vaupés. He did not reply or reprimand me. Later he came and talked to me. The life he lived and the certainty of his faith were new to me, and

I had not remembered any of this in my own background. I was interested.

"After many other visits from Leonel, I decided I wanted the kind of faith that he had. As a boy, I had given my life to Christ, but my religion consisted of the things I didn't do. I no longer danced in the devil dancing; I no longer smoked, drank, or chewed coca. I focused on good works, read my Bible and attended services regularly. But these things had no power to sustain me when I was tempted. It was all a show of how good I was, whereas inside I was rotten! I realized this after talking with Leonel—and I asked Jesus to forgive me. Forgive me He did, and He made me a new person! Now I want to live for Him and do the things that please Him. When I am tempted to do wrong, I know that He is with me to guide me. I have a purpose in life, and I know I am traveling up that narrow creek to Heaven, where I will be with God, my Creator and the Father of my Savior, Jesus Christ."

Placido finished and sat down. There was a profound silence. An Indian like themselves, he had challenged them to faith in God's salvation through Jesus Christ.

The stage of God's unfolding drama was being set. The previous night we had viewed the Triumphal Entry into Jerusalem, the Last Supper, and the Betrayal and Trial of Christ. On Thursday night, we repeated these and also showed the film on the Crucifixion. Placido also repeated his testimony, for the benefit of the forty new people who had arrived in time for the afternoon session.

I shall never forget Leonel's subsequent teaching on sin!

"What is sin?" he queried. No one looked up. No one answered. Finally Luis raised his hand. "Okay, Luis." Leonel pointed to him and encouraged him.

"Sin is when you have already accepted Christ into your life and then go and do something wrong," he said.

I wanted to hide! I was shocked, and looked down at the floor. "After all those years of teaching, and this is the basic part. How could he have missed it?" I thought.

No one else tried to answer. Luis realized he hadn't got it quite right and tried with something else just as devastating. In the few split seconds before Leonel spoke again, the Holy Spirit had to deal with me. "Is only your pride hurt, or is something greater at stake here?" I acknowledged to God that my pride was of little consequence.

"Lord, please enlighten them at this point of confusion," I silently prayed.

Leonel picked up the teaching again.

"Sin is believing the devil and not believing God," he said. "God told Adam and Eve in the Garden that if they ate of the tree of knowledge of good and evil they would surely die. But the devil came along and twisted God's words. 'Surely you will not die.' God has given us His laws, but we have the devil whispering in our ear, saying, 'Don't believe it.' If we choose to believe the devil and not God, we have chosen to sin."

After this allegory was over, Leonel challenged the people, "Whom will you choose to believe? Will you believe God and live, or believe the devil, the father of lies, and die?" His voice rose over the attentive audience. "Now, if Christ died for our sins, will He do it again if we sin again? No! Christ died once for all the sins of the world, past, present and future. Even if you have believed in Christ, and then listened to the devil and believed what he has told you, if you confess that sin, you are forgiven."

At that point, downcast heads were raised and ears were open to the words being spoken. Their hearts were encouraged as the Spirit of God penetrated the defenses raised by Satan in their burdened consciences.

God led Leonel on. "It does not matter what sins you have committed, or how bad you have been. Until you go over the great waterfall, you still have time to put fuel in your tank and get out of the river of sin. Confess your sins, and they will be forgiven."

How often had I said that in the past two and one-half years! They had not responded, but praise God, He was getting through to them now! Their guilt at having fallen so far from God and getting into the evils of the cocaine traffic was being lifted as they realized God would forgive them.

Friday evening saw an even bigger attendance. One hundred and twenty people crowded round to watch all three films, reliving and remembering the scenes they had watched the previous evening. All of them at one time or another had heard the story of the solemn and sad events of the scourging and crucifixion, but now they saw it unfold before their eyes. They were filled with awe, with shame, and with grief that their sins had caused Jesus to hang on that cross, with the nails through His hands. Some were filled with repentance. The vividness of it all was so overwhelming! Not a sound was heard as the awful episodes transfixed the audience. Soon the scenes would be removed from their eyes, but they would burn in their minds forever. All one hundred and twenty went home without a whisper. That night Nazareth lay in solemn silence as each person, lost in his own thoughts, drifted off to sleep.

Our middle daughter Becky, eight years old, came to us and asked Doreen to pray with her for salvation as we prepared for bed. What a glorious night for praise!

During Leonel's last day with us he felt that he should ask if anyone had received Christ as their personal Savior. The arms of two young men shot up, showing that they indeed had: Luis, a Barasano Indian man who had been flown in, and Javier, Luis Benjumea's son from our own tribe. Their faces glowed with the presence and peace of God.

Leonel asked again, "How many of you are sure after this week that you have a home awaiting in Heaven?"

Nine people stood up! Alberto was among them! Biviano was overjoyed! Once they were up, they felt a little self-conscious and a bit startled at what they had done. They looked from one to another and realized that together they were proclaiming God's church on the Caño Ti. They drew strength one from the other as they realized they were in this together with God. How we rejoiced in praise to God for this moment!

When everyone had left the next day, Biviano came to borrow the films. He wanted to take them to another village downriver to use them as a tool in evangelism. The confirmation God had been giving Biviano throughout the last year and the blessings God had given in this past week had left an indelible mark on his heart. Biviano could trust himself totally to God and do the ministry that God had called him to do. He was going off to minister with an enthusiasm and joy that he never had experienced before.

LOOKING DOWN
THE BARREL

It was three weeks since the Easter conference and three weeks since we had first heard about guerrilla activity in the Vaupés province. We contemplated our position, and realized that if the rebels were coming closer they were coming for us—because we were the only gringos (foreigners) left in the province! Wycliffe had pulled all their translators out of our area, to avoid another Chet Bitterman incident. It was over three years since he had been martyred in the capital, Bogotá, some four hundred miles from us.

We knew the local Indians were terrified of what would happen if the guerrillas came. They had seen horrifying pictures on the front pages of the newspaper of dead bodies lying in the streets after Communist guerrilla attacks. However, we had just spent eight years telling these people

God could take care of them. So now, at the hint of trouble, should we abandon them? Wouldn't that be hypocritical? On the other hand, wasn't our very presence there causing the danger of attack? We found it hard to decide what was the sensible and wise thing to do, both for ourselves and the newborn Carapana church.

We spent some time asking God for wisdom, and His answer came: "Stay!" I knew it clearly, but I was still concerned for my family. I didn't know what they might have to live through if I obeyed this clear command from God, and I hardly dared to contemplate what could happen to Doreen and our thirteen-year-old Amy at the hands of these ruthless men.

As Doreen and I continued to pray, more reports of guerrilla atrocities came in. Beti came to see us and told us how frightened the folks in her village were; already some had spent three days hiding in the jungle.

"Doreen," she said, "I am concerned about your safety."

"Beti, we know that God is in control and He will not forsake His people. Neither will He forsake the Carapana Indians. We need to stand firm for God if He tells us to," Doreen counseled her. "We cannot use arms against them, because they are much stronger than we are. Just be calm in their presence if they come."

Beti seemed much more relaxed when it was time for her to go. Little did Doreen realize how much she herself was going to need the advice she had given Beti! Beti had understood that God had sent her to warn and prepare us for what was coming—and in sharing so honestly with Beti, Doreen had been prepared by God for a right course of action.

Doreen put her arm around Beti, and Beti squeezed Doreen's arm as they parted—a very unusual display of affection on Beti's part; it is not their custom or a part of their culture to show emotion at all.

The following day Doreen came downstairs to the breakfast table and announced that God had spoken to her.

"What did He say?" I asked, feeling I already knew the answer.

"He said to stay, and that we would meet the guerrillas face to face and walk away from them," she replied. So along with this repeated command to stay came the assurance that everything would be all right.

I shared our conviction with Biviano that we should stay, and suggested that if the guerrilla forces came the villagers would be safer not to get involved. I also stressed our strong desire to see a church planted and growing among the Carapana. For that reason we would stay as long as we possibly could; but I asked Biviano if he felt the people were ready to lead the church themselves should we be forced to leave. He assured me that they were.

A week after God's revelation to Doreen, I decided that I had been overcautious in staying in or near the house all the time. We needed meat, and I felt that a night's fishing and hunting would give necessary relaxation. Everything seemed calm enough in our area, so Eddie and I packed the boat ready for a trip. It was a Saturday. We'd planned to leave at ten in the morning, but in God's overruling I decided to sit down and have a cup of coffee with Doreen first. While we were drinking our coffee, the motor in the washing machine stalled. The motor always made a terrible racket because it had no muffler. In the semi-silence I heard the motor of our little generator running, and realized I had forgotten to put it away after I'd charged up the battery which ran the bathroom light.

I walked out the side door and turned the generator off, and was still bent over it when a voice said, in Spanish, "Raise your hands!"

My mind took in the words, but they seemed so out of place that I turned around and replied, "What?" The command was repeated, and I found myself staring down the barrel of a 9mm machine gun! I quickly but carefully raised my hands and began walking towards the young man with the machine gun. I wanted to get him away from the house where my family was and out into the soccer field forty yards away. The man could see I had no gun, and was not running for help. As I looked at my captor and kept walking toward him, I noticed out of the corner of my eye that another uniformed man had already gone to the back of our house. On my right, a young woman armed with a large, lever-action rifle moved along the front of the village.

The motor of a boat became audible as one stopped at the dock in front of our house. More green-uniformed guerrillas poured into the village.

The guard in front of me barked a question. "Where are the rest of the men?"

"The Indians are either here in the village or working in their gardens," I replied.

"Not them," he corrected me. "The other Americans."

"There are no other Americans here except my family and me," I responded. "The others have been gone for nearly a month now."

"Where are your weapons?" he yelled.

"Over there," I motioned with my head as I spoke. "My son and I were on our way hunting. We have just a single-shot shotgun and a single-shot .22 rifle."

"Where is your cocaine?" was the next question.

"I have no cocaine," I replied. "I never took part in the cocaine trade. A cocaine trader lived in the village for a while, but he left six months ago."

"Call your family out!" the guard ordered. I turned to the house and called to Doreen to gather the children and come outside. We had company! As she came out, her face became grim as she looked at me with my hands up in front of a machine gun. The children were still in the front room of the house, playing. Doreen turned to call them and found them being marched through the front door by a guard. They ran to her and she drew them close. They were all marched out to join me. Their hands went up too, with Doreen hushing their questions.

We could hear the noise of the other guerrillas as they went through the house and the school—calling out to each other as they rummaged through our belongings.

Doreen, with the adrenaline pumping through her veins, told the children that she was going to pray. "God, I thank you that the blood of Jesus Christ surrounds us and protects us, and that nothing can cross over that blood line." Immediately the peace of God descended on us, and stayed with us throughout the whole ordeal.

As we continued to stand there, we wondered just who these people were. They could pass for Colombian soldiers or police—but their shoes were not uniform material. Some wore tennis shoes and others wore black rubber boots.

The guard questioned me, "Has the army been here lately?"

"No," I answered.

"Have the local police been here recently?"

"No," I said. "What would they want here?"

"Have there been guerrillas?" was the next demand.

"Why should they come here?" I chuckled as I replied. "There's nothing for them here."

We could hear people running through our house directly behind us, and then a boy of about fourteen came out with them. He was holding a machine gun and pointed it directly at us. The rest of the group had by this time lowered their guns or pointed them to one side, but this lad had a tormented, ugly look on his face and was obviously dangerous and demonic. He looked enviously at Eddie's hunting knife, and I thought for a moment he was going to take it from him. The boy was accompanied by an arrogant man who started to question me again about the matters the guard had already mentioned. This fellow was obviously the leader of the group. He was a short man, with a smirk on his face which defied anyone to question his authority. His mouth was somewhat deformed and his speech slurred, so I had difficulty in understanding what he said. I recognized that he was under demonic control.

That realization made me remember how Satan had provoked Herod to kill all the babies in Bethlehem, and Judas to betray the Lord Jesus. I took this as a challenge.

"God," I said in my spirit. "I pray for this man, that Satan will have no power or authority over him."

All except one guard then dispersed, and started going through our things again. It started to rain, soon becoming quite heavy, so I suggested to the guard that we move over to the house and find shelter under the lean-to roof where we kept our washing machine. He agreed, and although my family moved under cover, he stood resolutely against a banana plant in the rain. We moved over to make room for him and asked him to come in and keep dry. He was perplexed, not expecting this treatment! We should have been either terrified or angry, yet here we were, being considerate of him and discussing everyday affairs with him and with each other. We were the captives, and yet we seemed to be in calm control!

The rest of the group came back and gathered around us. They were clean cut and very cordial. Then the leader re-emerged and in his curt and surly manner asked me if I knew who they were.

"No, I don't know who you are," I replied.

"Aren't you curious?" he demanded.

"No," I replied with a smile. "I learned a long time ago that it is not wise to ask too many questions or to know too much."

"We are the EPL, a guerrilla group," he enlightened me. I didn't know of this group, but he thought it would frighten us to know they were guerrillas.

"We are here to take Colombia for the Colombians! We don't want any American capitalists exploiting our country. We don't want you in our country!" he shouted. The whole tirade increased in pitch and fervor as he spoke, but it was short-lived.

Suddenly he caught sight of our chickens (they are usually a precious commodity so far from civilization), and decided he was hungry and wanted one. I readily agreed to kill one for him. He looked shocked and stomped into the house. Looking around for the family, I saw them surrounded by five young men who were talking to them. One of them asked Amy how old she was, and I was immediately nervous. She was good-looking and appeared older than her thirteen years, but the bad moment passed.

The guerrillas sensed the well-hidden anxiety in the children, and assured them that they were not a bad group, they did not harm anyone, and did not intend to harm us. We relaxed a bit at that, although we found out later that they were not EPL at all, but a much more militant group, the FARC, which had already kidnapped three Americans that year.

About noon, the leader came and asked me to show him how to operate our ham radio. I followed him into the house.

"Would you and your people like something to eat?" I asked. "My wife could cook you a meal."

"No!" he almost screamed. "She would probably poison it."

"Sir," I said, "the Son of God, whom we serve, came to save, not to kill."

He looked at me in alarm and then backed away with a hysterical cackle, bumping into one of the woman guerrillas. She quickly withdrew from him with a look of terror on her face at his behavior, but he soon controlled his laughter and tried to rally himself. The most he could utter were a few incoherent sentences, trying to make fun of me, but he signaled the girl to watch Doreen and make something to eat.

When we headed upstairs to our bedroom where the radio was kept, I asked, "Do you want to learn how the radio works, so that you can use it when you take it away?" He looked at me, and tried to deny that he had any intention of taking it. At that point another boat arrived. It had been sent away earlier to report our capture, and also to take the fourteen-year-old boy away. He had obviously added danger to their situation. We saw that the Lord was working in our behalf.

I showed the leader and another young guerrilla with him how to use the radio. The younger man was very intelligent, but seemed to have no position of command in the group. He was well educated and had come from a much more cultured part of the country. I went over the procedure with the leader, but he could not grasp how to use the radio. This seemed to disgust the younger fellow, but he said nothing. Then the leader picked up my camera and asked questions about that. He asked how to operate it and took a picture of the wall! The young recruit had had enough of the uncouth leader's behavior and seemed clearly apologetic about it. He excused himself and went downstairs.

Next I was asked to turn on and operate the radio. But before I could do that I had to go off to connect the antenna and start up the generator. Coming down the stairs, I saw Doreen and Amy baking bread in the kitchen, and making a meal for our family. The other children were in the living room, reading and talking to the guerrillas. I connected the antenna and started the generator, and went back upstairs to explain over and over again the procedure for tuning the radio.

Part of the leader's motive was to irritate me so that I would get angry and lose control; then he could justifiably retaliate in any way he pleased. We had been memorizing Scripture as a family on Sunday mornings, and a recently memorized verse was Proverbs 15:1, "A soft answer turns away wrath, but grievous words stir up anger." Once again we could see how God had been preparing us.

The commander also tried to catch me in a lie—by cross-examining me on any remark I had made to the other guerrillas, who promptly reported it back to him.

He was very impressed with the radio, but eventually told me to turn it off, and headed off to rejoin the others. I asked again if they were hungry, and offered to get two chickens so that the whole team could have a meal. He agreed this time, and I went off to the schoolroom to get some corn to attract the chickens. I knew real temptation in that schoolroom as I looked at my shotgun and my pocketful of shotgun shells! A guerrilla had been assigned to accompany me to the schoolhouse, but he hadn't come inside. The moment soon passed, and I went out to lure the two nearest chickens to their death. I beheaded them, and a second guerrilla was assigned to clean them. In the house I found all the other guerrillas exclaiming in delight over Doreen's fresh-baked bread. We ate our soup as a family, and as Doreen cleared up she offered the guard who was guarding her some rice to go with the chickens and bread.

One guerrilla had unearthed our tape recorder in his fresh search of the house, and he started playing it. We had left a tape in—of Scripture choruses in song— and although he did not understand the English words, he saw we were enjoying it so he played it over and over again. How those words ministered to us as a family! God used them to remind us again of His protection.

When I was led outside again to disconnect the radio antenna, the leader followed me and started to interrogate me. Where was our money? How did we get it? Where was all the fancy equipment which Americans were supposed to have? What job did my father do, since he could afford to visit me so often? They had obviously done some intelligence research before their visit! After his questioning, he wrote out a report and went off to send it by boat back to base camp.

Back in the house I got into conversation with one young man and was able to tell him why we were not afraid and about our God and Protector. When he had finished eating and moved away, I was joined by the young fellow who had played the tape for us. I tried to witness to him too, but he quickly turned his conversation to their "cause," becoming more frantic and fanatical as he went on—but ceasing abruptly when the others returned.

The group had tired of looking through our belongings and were bored. They weren't allowed to take anything until the leader could have his pick, so all but those on guard duty had come in to talk. I started to share with the younger men, but as soon as I spoke the leader started to denounce American idealism, capitalism and intervention. I made a comment which included the word "Communism" and immediately realized my mistake. The leader bristled with fury, and it was then that I learned that the leaders were trained Communists and the rest were slowly being indoctrinated into what they knew only as "the cause." I was on dangerous ground, and had to do some verbal acrobatics to get onto something less controversial.

My boots were the next topic of conversation. They were military boots, and they wanted to know how I got them. I just might be a soldier! I explained that someone in America had once given them to me, and I had brought them with me to Colombia in case they would be of use. We had not told them any lies, and we had answered all their questions. Our answers so far had tied up with their advance research on us—but they had to be sure about the boots, in case they had been misinformed!

Eventually the group left the house again and we were alone with one guard. I began to ask him about how their "cause" was going, and the length of time he would be committed to this kind of action.

"Until we win," he promptly replied.

"How long until you take over the country?" I asked.

"Well, we are nearer our goal now," he explained.

I continued to probe. "What is standing in your way? You are well armed and well organized."

With considerable bitterness he blurted out, "We could take Colombia today—and its army—but with you gringos here, your country would soon put a finger in. We can't beat both of them." The conversation was over.

A new man arrived when one of the boats came back from base camp. He went straight upstairs to see the radio. During the day we had counted fifteen different guerrillas, and two were women in their early twenties. One of them was leaning against our doorway now, watching some of the others play tetherball. I remarked that their times of relaxation and enjoyment must be few and far between. She told us that life at base camp was fine, and that things on the field were not too tough. She showed genuine interest in us and asked how we could raise our children so far from civilization.

It was now getting dark, and the group had talked of leaving, but they were still around . . . and even while playing games had their guns ready. The leader and the new man who had been looking at the radio came back from their inspection. The new man was of equal or even higher rank, and suddenly called attention to the first leader's boots. Mine!

"Is he wearing your boots?" he asked.

"Yes, he is," I replied. "How do they fit?"

"Oh fine," the first leader said, caught off guard.

"I'm glad they fit you, and that you can make use of them," I said with a smile. "They never did fit me very well."

The men standing around started to chuckle as they realized that the two leaders' taunts had gotten no reaction. The man in my boots tried to regain his authority. "It's only right that I wear them. I am military and you are not!" His tone was belittling, but the impact of his words was already lost.

"Your children sure have blond hair," the second leader commented.

I explained that my wife and I had both been blond as children, but that our hair had got darker as we grew older. I also commented on my lack of hair, pointing to my bald patch, and suggested I should borrow some from one of the guerrillas who had a mop of hair! At this, the group laughed loudly, some of the tension having been dispelled. I continued to connect up the radio antenna again.

As I looked up from that task, I saw Biviano, Alberto and a few others sitting across the village watching us. They felt so despairing and helpless about our plight, and I hoped that hearing the laughter from our house would relieve some of their fears. After I'd fixed the generator I went into the house and sat on the sofa. Becky came up and sat beside me. She put her arms around me and gave me a big hug.

"Isn't it nice that Jesus has His big,

loving arms around us?" she asked. I could only reply with a hug, the answer was so obvious. Jesus most certainly had! Although we were nervous and under strain, we sensed an overwhelming peace and assurance that allowed us to interact with our captors and share God's love with them. Although they hated what they thought we stood for—American capitalism—they were drawn to us and interested in us as individuals. Some of them told us about their own wretched childhood, as they felt God's love flow out to them. We had opportunity to share at length with them.

Our family was together in the living room: Doreen keeping herself busy with sewing; Eddie playing checkers with one of the guerrillas, a hard-core Communist; Amy reading a story to five-year-old Cheryl. Suddenly the front door opened and I was ordered out to the church building to meet the leaders. I was escorted there in the darkness, but the escort left me at the door, and I walked over to the leaders. They told me to sit down—and again the interrogation started up. All the old questions. All the old answers. There was some new information for us though. Although originally coming just to intimidate us, the leaders were now thinking of kidnapping us! (Didn't they know that no one pays ransom for missionaries?) The darkness was oppressive, and they were about to say something more when they changed their minds.

"We have more to discuss with you but will first go and listen to the radio," the new leader informed me.

We returned to the house—and more instructions about the use of the radio. The new man knew more than the other, but was not familiar with this model—he made my head ache as he moved the dial back and forth incessantly, not stopping to listen to any instructions. My back ached, too, from sitting on the bed without any support. Then I noticed the guerrilla's machine gun on the bed cover beside me! Another moment of temptation—but I didn't know how to use his machine gun. At last they told me to turn the radio off, and we all trooped back downstairs to the living room.

"It is time for you to go to bed," the leaders declared. "We will talk again in the morning."

"Are you leaving?" we inquired.

"No," came the firm reply.

"You have no sleeping gear with you," I observed. "You will find hammocks and blankets in the barrels in the schoolhouse. And you can take these cushions from the sofa. Make yourselves comfortable."

We went upstairs to bed, and in no

time the children were sound asleep. Doreen and I reviewed the events of the day—something we did every night. Both of us felt that two of the guerrillas seemed very familiar, and it was Doreen who remembered that they were two of three young fellows with whom I'd played basketball only six months before, while they were "visiting" Nazareth. They had obviously been spying out the land.

We reviewed God's goodness to us, and how thankful we were that the children had handled each situation so well. I told Doreen of the way I'd been able to witness to two of the men, and she shared about her conversation with the three who had guarded her and how another one had deliberately tried to irritate and antagonize her by messing up her spotlessly clean and tidy kitchen!

Finally, I felt I had to share with her the possibility of my being kidnapped. I said I would be ready to go the next morning, hoping the family would be spared. But even that possibility was agonizing, and we spent the rest of the night wrapped in our own thoughts and prayers, wondering what tomorrow would hold.

RUN, CHILDREN, RUN

We held our breath as heavy boots trudged across the floor downstairs. The guerrilla on patrol had come in the front door, gone through the ground floor, and left by the side door. We breathed again. The night was dark and so long, filled with anguish and prayers. I dozed lightly. Doreen moved in the bed and it woke me up. She was feeling sick, but seemed to settle down a bit when I rubbed her back.

Back came the footsteps. In at the front door, around the staircase and out the side door. It was a regular routine patrol, and there was no hope for sleep. Doreen was sick again. A baby cried in a nearby Indian house. Becky snored for a while. Still the night would not end.

Finally, a distant gray began to lighten the sky, and people stirred as dawn approached. It was Sunday morning. Downstairs the guerrillas moved in and out of the house. The children began to wake up and come into our room. Hoping that I alone would be accepted as a hostage, letting the family go free, I chose clothes which would last a long time, filling my pockets with my eyeglasses, a spare set of contact lenses, contact solution, and a small pocketknife. We heard footsteps coming up the stairs. It was the leader of the guerrillas, but it was still too dark to see his face clearly. His voice was easily recognizable however.

"Did you sleep well?" he asked.

Doreen had had enough of this and replied to the ridiculous question with a curt, "No!"

"Oh," replied the man. "The rain must have kept you awake."

Before we could say any more, he ordered me to loosen the antenna wire and extension cord of the radio. They were wrapped around a post, and when I had loosened them, he went downstairs and began pulling them down. We gathered at the foot of the bed with the children and, somehow managing not to cry, we prayed together asking God to keep us throughout the day.

There was a lot of movement downstairs, and the men seemed to be carrying off more and more of our goods. Then a motor started up, and a boat went downriver towards their base camp. We looked at each other, and I put my eye to a crack in the wall. I could see only four guerrillas, but one of them was one I considered "hard core." I suggested we go down and have breakfast. The guerrillas were busy shooting with my .22 caliber rifle. It made us nervous!

We made breakfast, and just as we were about to sit down and eat, another motor started up and a second boat took off downriver. Again we looked at each other questioningly, mentally noting that at one time there had been three boats. How many had stayed the night? Was one still around? Our questions were soon answered as Alberto came running over to our house, calling my name. He told us that all the guerrillas had gone! We stared in disbelief. It couldn't be true! But when we flocked outside there wasn't any guerrilla boat to be seen. Could the whole ordeal really be over?

In a daze, we talked to Alberto and some of the other Indians, asking how they had fared. Together we went over to the schoolhouse and looked at the school books and papers which had been strewn about and trampled on. Over a thousand dollars worth of brand new books had been stored there. It was obvious that a great deal of what hadn't been destroyed had been stolen.

We all went wearily back to the house

and sat down to our cool porridge. The guerrillas had not told us to leave, but perhaps it would be wise and would ease the pressure on our Indian friends. When should we leave? Doreen was ready to leave that day, but we decided to go during the coming week.

We began making a list of things we valued most . . . things we wanted to take. Only the most precious items could go. Amy wanted her white Bible and her music box, Eddie his hunting knife, Becky and Cheryl their dolls, Doreen the album with pictures of the children at each year of their lives. We knew the rest of the basic packing list for traveling, so we turned our thoughts back to the present.

On Sundays we always memorized a Bible verse and I had an idea of one I wanted for this Sunday. I leafed through the concordance to find it.

"For thou hast been a shelter for me, and a strong tower from the enemy" (Psalm 61:3).

Assurance, peace, relief, and an overwhelming sense of God's presence flooded over me. I laid my head on the table and wept with relief and joy, saying, "Thank You, Jesus! Thank You, Jesus!" This alarmed the children, but Doreen soon calmed them down. They had tears in their eyes too, knowing as vividly as Doreen and I what we had all faced during the past twenty-four hours. We had prayed many times as a family for other folks kidnapped as hostages in Colombia that year: first a Texaco businessman, and then Russel Stendel and Ricky Kirby whom we knew personally. None of these were missionaries, and ransom had been paid for them. It was an understood principle that ransom would not be paid for missionaries like Chet Bitterman and ourselves. So many missionaries work in dangerous and isolated places, and their vulnerability would quickly escalate the kidnapping trade if ransom were to be paid.

THE GUERILLAS RETURN

The children were anxious to be off, and when they had been excused they ran out to play with their Indian friends. Doreen and I sat at the table a while longer and then got up to do some necessary chores. While she cleaned up in the kitchen, I went outside to hide another ten gallons of gasoline. When I finished, I noticed a group of Indians walking towards me. They were from another village, and their presence in Nazareth puzzled me, but at the time I did not stop to analyze the situation. These people knew we had been captured by the guerrillas, but they had no way of knowing that the guerrillas had left. I began talking to them in front of our house, and Amy came out in her bathing suit, saying she was going down to the river for a bath. Just as she said that, I heard a motor downriver. It seemed far off, but since we had lived in the jungle our hearing had become exceptionally acute.

"There goes a motor on the Vaupés River," I said to the young man with whom I'd been talking.

"No," he replied, "that motor is on our river."

"Oh, I don't think so. It sounds too far away," I countered—but even as I spoke reality flooded over me! The guerrillas had used some sort of silencer on their boats, and they were returning. In fact they were very near!

"Doreen! They are coming back! Amy, get dressed!" I shouted.

"I'm not waiting here for them," cried Doreen, anguish in her voice. "Cheryl, Cheryl, come quick!"

By now our other children were with us in front of the house, and Cheryl appeared from Alberto's house—but without her shoes. I scooped her up, and we began to run for the jungle behind the house. The route we took would lead us to another village, if we could find and follow the little-used path. As we ran into the jungle I said to myself, "No! No! This is not the way it should be. We should turn back and wait. We should not provoke them."

But all the time I felt as if a force bigger than myself was pushing me from behind.

Two visiting Indian women, from the village to which this path led, were running into the jungle with us. They were part of the group which had recently appeared in Nazareth, and they called out to us that they were going back home. Once I had let them leave, I had second thoughts! I was not sure I could find the path on my own as I had never used it before. I took my family deep into the jungle, and we hid behind the outstretched roots of a large tree.

The minutes dragged by and the mosquitos tormented us. Our ears strained for sounds, and the leaves seemed to rustle noisily whenever we shifted our weight or moved. Would they come into the jungle and look for us? How many had returned? After half an hour, a motor started up and moved down the Caño Ti out of hearing. Had they really left? Were there any guards still in Nazareth? Ten minutes later I heard my name being called. It was Alberto's voice and he was on the path by which we'd entered the jungle. I did not answer back—afraid that it was a trick. Perhaps there was a guerrilla walking behind him with a machine gun. Alberto turned back down the path. Then we heard others calling our names in the distance, along other paths. Checking the path where Alberto had been, I saw only one set of footprints. He had been alone.

The time had come for us to leave the Carapana area, and we went together to the edge of the jungle near the village. Leaving the family about a hundred yards down another trail to wait for me, I cautiously worked my way from one patch of brush to another, trying to keep hidden from sight. Finally I reached the side of Biviano's house and stood outside, listening to the Indians talking inside. Their conversation reassured me that no guerrillas were in the village, so I stepped inside. Several of the Indians jumped when they saw me. Everyone was on edge. Here, too, were Indians from another village. Why were they here? I was judging everything in the light of the current tension, and it was only a letter we received six months later that finally answered this particular question. They, and the other Indians who had fled, had come to attend our Sunday service!

After greeting the other Indians, I started to fire one question after another at Biviano—without stopping for a reply! "What did the guerrillas have to say? How many were there? When are they coming back?"

He ignored the first question. "There were three," he said. "And I told them you had gone for a family walk and might not be back until 2 P.M. They were very angry not to find you here," he added urgently. "You must get away to Mitú!"

"Yes, I believe it will be better for you if we leave now," I said. "We are causing you unnecessary danger. Don't be saddened by what is taking place. You know that we were here purposely to plant a church among you. You and I believe that you, Biviano, are capable of carrying it on now," I reminded him.

"Yes," said Biviano, before I could say more. "Yes, we will carry on the church."

"I believe you will," I assured him. "Now could you please borrow Luis's canoe and Alberto's motor? If I take my own, the guerrillas will soon notice that it's missing. In the jungle next to the soccer field I've hidden food and gasoline. Put them in the boat along with some paddles and sheets of plastic—then hide the canoe in the creek by my garden. I'll bring my family from the jungle and we will leave when it is dark. Don't stay anywhere near the creek, or the guerrillas will know you helped us. Come back quickly and then take whatever you want from our house. The guerrillas will steal everything when they return."

I yelled goodbye to everyone and ran back to our house to collect some things for the family. I grabbed a basket and filled it with enough food for a few meals, putting a sheet of plastic over the food. I noticed that one of the trunks had been left open, after the guerrillas had ransacked the place, and there was the photo album which was so precious to Doreen! I scooped it up and walked through the house. It was in such disarray. I felt lonely! In our bedroom I found my wallet. The twenty dollars was gone, but my identification papers were still there. I looked around at our other belongings and decided that there was nothing other than my Bible that would help us. Back downstairs, I took a machete from a hook on the wall as I left the house.

I rejoined the family not more than twenty minutes after I had left them. As I showed Doreen the things I had brought, she realized that I had forgotten Cheryl's shoes, and that her own ID papers were still back in her wallet in the house! I still had time to get them. Sending the family deeper into the jungle, I raced back to the house, grabbed Doreen's wallet—and remembered that she had not taken a sweater, and we found the jungle nights cold. I looked longingly at my camera! I couldn't take it, as that would betray the fact that we had been back to the village. I found Cheryl's shoes and some insect repellant and ran back to the family.

We repacked the hastily filled basket,

and then set off due west in order to reach the path I thought we should take. Instead of reaching the path, we came to a deep ravine which we had no idea existed! I went on alone and scouted again for the right path. Thinking I'd found it, I retraced my steps to the family. As we moved along my chosen route, I noticed some fresh tracks which crossed our own. Looking at them closely, I realized that they were our own! We had gone round in a complete circle!

Once more I went on alone to search for the right trail, but within a hundred yards I had lost even our own tracks— while trying to find our starting point! The sun was hot, and I was exhausted and despairing. I was grateful that Doreen was doing such a good job of keeping the children calm, but my nerves were strained from concentrating on finding the path and listening for the return of that dreaded motor.

"God, look what a mess I am making out of this!" I said to my Heavenly Father.

His answer was soft. "I will be the One who takes you out of this."

Suddenly I saw the path in front of me—and I hadn't even moved! It was indeed the path on which we had started our tangled tour. I led the family down it, retracing our steps to the village. We went along the village clearing, casting fearful but wistful glances at our old house. We then followed a path to our garden by the creek, and there was the canoe which Biviano had cleverly hidden. It was neatly packed with paddles, motor, gasoline, and food. Paddling the canoe back upcreek about a hundred yards into the jungle, we got out, spread out plastics we had taken, and settled down to rest and await nightfall. Doreen opened a can of peaches for us—a welcome treat.

Thoughts started jumping around in my mind. "We haven't enough food to survive in the jungle for long. We've camped in the jungle before, but we had better supplies than these. If we stay hidden for a few days, maybe this nightmare will pass. To try to go down the river will only expose us to the guerrillas. Besides, they will have the mouth of the Caño Ti well guarded, waiting for us. But where else can we go?"

Doreen and I talked for a while, commenting again on how well the children were handling the situation. Then we lapsed into silence.

Back jumped my ideas! "The guerrillas have not returned, and it is well past two o'clock. Perhaps they will not come. I could slip back and get more food, more adequate supplies. I would easily hear their motor if the guerrillas did return, and have time to make a getaway. Plenty of time. I could . . ."

My heart stopped! My ears strained! We all sat up and huddled close together. The motors were coming! We could see the river from the canopy of leaves where we were hidden, but knew we could not be seen. It was imperative, though, to keep absolutely still and not make a sound. We waited as the motor approached, the familiar sound confirming that it was one of the powerful guerrilla boats. A quarter of a mile, an eighth of a mile, one more bend in the river. . . . There! We saw guns bristling from both sides of their boat as the men looked upriver to their objective— our village! Nazareth was only a quarter of a mile away. The boat passed from view, and almost immediately another one appeared. We huddled down into awed silence.

My heart cried out, "God! This isn't a game any more. If they find us now, I don't know what they will do." Then hope poured into me. "Father, I don't know where they are, but You have children who know how to pray. Will You wake some of them up and have them start praying? Thank You."

Peace again enveloped me, but the facts of the situation were still inescapable. We moved deeper into the valley to hide, and God began to drop ideas into my mind which led to one logical conclusion, and to positive direction. There had originally been three guerrilla boats. Two had just returned to Nazareth, of which one had undoubtedly continued on to the Wycliffe airstrip to see if we had managed to reach there. The guerrillas in Nazareth would not move until they had received information from the airstrip—and that could take some time. But I wondered about some of the Indians in Nazareth; there were those who, if threatened with a gun, might betray us. I decided to move, just in case they were forced into giving us away. It was only 4:30 in the afternoon, an hour and a half before nightfall. The river was low at this time of the year too. Not only would we be visible to any passing boat, but there would not be much chance of moving off the main channel of the Caño Ti to hide. We would be sitting ducks! But the insistent urge from the Lord was to *move!*

DEPARTURE

Obedience to God is always more reliable than any logic, so we piled into the boat and paddled further downstream from Nazareth. Our ears strained for the sound of a motor, but we paddled silently until we reached a creek three hundred yards down the river. We could get in only a little way, because the entrance was blocked by fallen logs, so we had to rely on the surrounding foliage for scant cover. We all sat silent and still. Every move or wiggle resulted in what sounded like a loud, loud noise, and the slightest movement of the canoe sent waves out into the main stream of the river. It was quite possible that the guerrillas would force one of our villagers to bring them silently downriver in a canoe to look for us, and our presence could so easily be betrayed by the slightest move.

It was easy to calculate the distance to the next spot where we could take refuge. The uncertain factor was the possibility of a guerrilla boat coming by on the river before we reached that refuge! The tension was incredible, and every fiber of my being was tingling with apprehension. Keeping silent, listening for an approaching motor, and paddling as fast as possible were the only factors we could consciously control as we set off and made for our next hiding place. We reached the creek safely, and were able to travel up and around three bends into a place where no guerrilla boat could reach. There even our loudest noises would not be heard out on the river.

Getting out of the canoe, we quickly spread out plastics and put out a few items in readiness for the fast-falling night. We stretched out, and Doreen opened a can of sardines and a can of crackers. They were devoured eagerly, but not very tidily, and crumbs fell from our fingers onto the plastic. This brought an ever-increasing stream of ants which also did some biting. Six-year-old Cheryl was in their direct line of travel and she couldn't handle it, but they soon became too much for us all! There was only one solution: to get into the canoe and try to rest there.

Within minutes we were packed and into the canoe, but it took longer to kill off all the ants which had come into the canoe via our bodies. While we had been eating, the storm we had been expecting passed over us in a flurry of wind and cloud, but there was no rain. Now that we were in the canoe, it seemed silly to just sit there, so we decided to move on downriver. Darkness had arrived. A mile further down was a creek which led to a house the Indians had formerly used in their old days of collecting crude rubber. I was toying with the idea of going there to sit out this crisis.

When we got out of the creek and into the main stream of the Caño Ti, the night was clear, but thankfully there was no moon to highlight our escape. As we paddled down the river this time we were a bit more relaxed. I reminded Doreen of how reluctant the guerrillas had been to leave the village after dark the night before. That seemed such a long time ago! A few mental calculations led me to realize that their base camp was probably not on the Caño Ti, but more probably upstream on the Vaupés River. We would be traveling on downstream, but caution dictated that we should paddle down the Vaupés for a considerable distance before it would be safe to use our motor.

We passed the creek which led to the Indian rubber-collecting house and were three-quarters of the way to the Vaupés River, but I could go no further. We had traveled for two-and-a-half hours. Directing the canoe into a creek, I fell asleep sitting up with my head resting on the paddle. The younger children fell asleep too.

Forty minutes later I awoke, feeling somewhat rested, but still with this compulsive urge to keep moving. It was as though God were pushing us on, hurrying us out of there. The thought of what still lay ahead was very intimidating. We had to go through the mouth of the Caño Ti and into the Vaupés. The Caño Ti was only forty yards wide at that point, with a fishing camp on one bank. The forty-yard stretch was clearly visible at night, and I was sure that the guerrillas would have that third boat strategically placed there to block our escape. Nearer and nearer we paddled to the ominous spot. Eddie,

Becky and Cheryl were lying asleep in the bottom of the canoe. Doreen and Amy were helping to paddle, but as we approached the last turn I whispered to them to lie down too. I would paddle the canoe through alone.

With an urgent prayer I guided the canoe to the side of the river opposite to the fishing camp, hugging the shadow of the bank, and avoiding logs which stuck out into the river. I was grateful for the practice I had had in paddling silently at night on my fishing trips. We were now abreast of the fishing camp, but I could see no sign of life.

A loud snore suddenly rent the air! Horror filled my heart and I waited for a bullet to strike or for someone to challenge us—but nothing happened. Doreen could not reach Becky, so she poked her with her paddle. Becky turned over, and the snoring stopped! We all breathed a sigh of relief as we left another danger spot behind us.

Praise God, we were on our way to safety! We crossed the Vaupés River and went along the shadowed bank on the far side. After half an hour it started to rain and we covered the sleeping children with the plastic. Doreen and I took off our outer clothes—tucking them under the plastic to keep them dry. When the rain stopped, we put back on our dry, warm clothes and went on!

On and on we paddled, until we reached the place where it was safe to use our motor and make better speed, but I was too tired to continue. As we entered another creek to rest it started to pour rain again, so we all huddled under the plastic. I dozed.

Some time later Amy woke me, complaining that she was sitting in water. Sleepily, I cupped my hand and began scooping up water and throwing it in the air. I thought I was bailing water out of the canoe, but was too drowsy to realize that it was going straight up and coming back into the canoe. I fell more deeply asleep, and it was half an hour later that Amy woke me again—in real alarm! The water was still coming into the canoe and threatening to sink it. That did wake me! Grabbing the flashlight, I shone it around to discover the canoe had lowered in the river because of the extra weight of the rain water inside of it. The water outside the canoe was only three inches from the top of the canoe, and we were about to be submerged in the fifteen-foot-deep river! I scooped the water out as rapidly as I could and the danger was averted, but I was thoroughly wet and very cold. Wrapping myself in plastic to keep warm, I took up the paddle again. Everyone changed position to be more comfortable, and we paddled the canoe back into the Vaupés River. Then I put the motor in place and started it.

Traveling on a river by motorboat at night is like hurtling through a tunnel with jagged edges reaching out to get you. The sky is a lighter hue than the trees on the bank, so you keep in the lighter reflection on the water, just off the shadows cast by the trees. All the time you have to be on the alert for a fallen tree which may reach out into the river, and you determine the course of the river by watching the skyline of the trees.

At the first streak of dawn, we searched for another creek in which to hide. We soon found one, but it was blocked by fallen trees. We docked the canoe and got out, but I was not happy. We were too close to the main river in order to be well hidden. Trying to make the best of the situation, we cleared a small spot and tried to get a fire going. We were all soaking wet, and the children were shivering as they tried to wring out their clothes. It is always difficult to light a fire in the damp jungle, but after a downpour like the one we had had it was almost impossible. Doreen rummaged in our supplies and found a candle which kept enough constant heat on the twigs to get them lit, but to our consternation the heavy smoke drifted out to the Vaupés

River. Doreen also got out some food, and then we realized that everything we had brought needed to be cooked, and we had nothing to cook it in! We finally made a meal of a can of peanuts and a can of raisins.

The fire warmed up, the smoke subsided, and we relaxed a little. I boiled some coffee in the empty peanut can while the children dried their clothes by the fire. Doreen lay down on the plastic and in seconds was fast asleep. As I thought about our situation, an unexpected and exhilarating sense of joy filled me. We did not have a thing in this world that anyone could take away from us. We did not own a thing! We were totally dependent on God, and what a warm feeling it was to trust Him implicitly. Doreen woke refreshed after fifteen minutes, and as she drank some hot coffee we joked together about how little it really takes to keep body and soul together.

THE NIGHTMARES END

The morning was overcast, and again God gave me that inner compulsion to keep moving—this time downriver to Mitú, a ninety-mile journey. We got back into the canoe and, praying silently, headed off. We used the motor now as it was vital to move quickly. At midmorning we passed a village where the Indians were lining the riverbank to watch us go by. They waved, as most of them knew us. I pulled nearer to the shore.

"Have the guerrillas been here yet?" I asked.

"No!" came their startled reply.

"We're from the Caño Ti, and we've just escaped from them," I called. "We don't want them to know we passed this way."

Others were arriving from the village to hear what was going on, and by the general excitement and the rapid retreat of the whole band, we knew we need have no worries about them. They would disappear into the jungle and no one would see them for days. It was a relief to know that the guerrillas had not reached this far.

An hour later we came to those crucial Mandí rapids. From our first trip we had always regarded Mandí as a vulnerable spot, and the villagers had become increasingly hostile towards "gringos" and increasingly influenced by militant Communism. Doreen's fear of the rapids was greater than her fear of the Mandí Indians, however, and I negotiated the canoe through the rapids alone while she walked through the village with the children. They quickly got back into the canoe beyond the rapids, thankful that no one had seen them. Just as we were pulling out, a man ran to the bank and called out. He had recognized me, and wanted to ask about a relative in the Caño Ti. I answered his questions from a safe distance, telling him that we had just escaped from the guerrillas and dare not delay.

We came to the Cubéo Christian village where we had often been given hospitality, but we passed on, not wanting our presence to endanger them. At 2:30 P.M. on Monday, May 21, we arrived at Mitú. The place where we usually docked was owned by a relative of some Caño Ti Indians, and often folks from our river would visit there. They came to the dock when we arrived, startled at our ragged and exhausted state. We explained briefly what had happened, and the Indians helped us carry some of our things to the house of Feliciano and Elsy Velasco, fine Colombian Christians who had always hosted us on our visits to Mitú.

As Feliciano came out to greet us, he too exclaimed at our appearance, and again I gave a brief account of our escape from the guerrillas. Feliciano swayed backwards as I told him the story, reaching out a hand to steady himself. He said they had been praying for us for three days, and that each night he had had a nightmare in which men in green uniforms chased him from tree to tree. Every time he woke from this dream, God had prompted him to pray for us! He had taken part in our sufferings, and God had answered my prayer on the riverbank, that He would prompt some of His children to pray for us. We have since received over a dozen letters from people who had been led to intercede for us during those days, even though they knew nothing of our circumstances at the time.

Once the whole family had moved up to the house, and the canoe was locked up so that Luis could recover it later, I decided to report our escape to the local army unit. While I was at their headquarters, Elsy told Doreen that the guerrillas were threatening to shoot anyone who told the army of their movements. The military personnel were exasperated when they learned about our capture in the northwest of the province. The guerrillas had staged a clever diversion to the south to draw the army down there, and meanwhile the rebel troops had poured into the north until now the capital city of the province was cut off and surrounded by guerrillas.

One local official suggested that we should have a guard for the night, as no planes were leaving Mitú until the following day. The commander refused, but later we saw a group of soldiers at each corner of the block. We were so exhausted that it didn't matter. Nothing would keep us from sleeping that night!

As soon as the government office opened the next morning, we inquired about getting a plane out of the jungle. The province was officially declared under siege, and only a few planes were allowed to enter or leave the town each day. No plane came that morning—but it seemed that all the residents of Mitú did! On some pretext or other, they all went past the door to see the "gringos" who had escaped from the guerrillas. This made us uneasy and fearful of reprisals from the guerrillas in a face-saving move. Finally at two in the afternoon we were given passage on a plane, along with twelve other people. Our loving Colombian co-workers paid for our flight out.

Usually several policemen checked passengers at the plane. Today, surprisingly, there was only one. We learned the reason for that as we took off. The rest were concealed around the airstrip perimeter—expecting a guerrilla attack!

We gradually relaxed on the flight. Once the immediate tension oozed away, we began to take stock of our fellow passengers. One was a scientist who had the plane well stocked with cages of bats! I talked to him for a while, and, scanning the other people idly, presumed there was nobody we knew. Then Eddie saw one face which he knew and became ill at recognizing it. We were sure that he was correct.

As we neared our destination, a little airstrip at the very foot of the Andes Mountains, with no lights or control tower, a violent thunderstorm broke. The pilot, who flew by sight and few instruments, could see nothing. The men on the plane began to panic, but suddenly the pilot saw a gap in the clouds, turned the plane on its side, got through the hole and landed! God still had His hands on us.

When the plane door opened, we were greeted by seven army soldiers. I walked over to the fellow whose face Eddie had recognized in the plane.

"Where did we see you before?" I asked.

"In Mitú, no doubt," he mumbled.

"No, I haven't been there for eighteen months," I said. Then I smiled as I reminded him of our last encounter. "I played basketball with you on October the twelfth at Nazareth on the Caño Ti!"

He blanched, looking out of the door at the soldiers and then back at me. He was the third man of the guerrilla spy-out-the-land party who had been to the Caño Ti more than six months ago, and had obviously been detailed to follow us from Mitú! Knowing he was recognized, he was terrified that I would turn him in to the waiting soldiers. But we did not want to risk further clashes with the guerrillas which could cause retaliation on our Indian friends in the Caño Ti region, so we boarded a bus and went to the orphanage in Villavicencio. The guerrilla boarded with us, but jumped out of the bus after two-hundred yards, and raced back to the terminal in the pouring rain.

For six weeks after we arrived in Villavicencio, nightmares persisted as we thought of all the things that could have gone wrong. Then, as the nightmares passed, we began to think and pray about our future ministry in Colombia. We could continue in a "safe" area and still work among Indians. Keeping in touch with Leonel and Belgica, we began to make plans for staying in Villavicencio, fully confident that God must want us here. We decided that we would take a furlough and then return to Colombia.

GOD'S PLAN ACCOMPLISHED

After we had been home for four months, continuing to wait on God for His plan and timing, He spoke to us quietly and gently telling us that we would not be returning. He had guided us to plant a church on the Caño Ti, and now He was guiding us to stay in the U.S.A. Why? It was such a shock. We had never realized that our good-bye to our Indian friends had been anything but temporary. But it was undeniably God's voice, guiding us once more against the logic of our own thinking and desires. It has cost a lot to obey, but we have His peace as we continue in obedience. We are currently serving as Midwest Regional Representatives for our mission, WEC International. We share with churches and Bible schools in America the challenge of Jesus' last command, to take the gospel to those who have never heard.

News from the Caño Ti has been scarce, but we did learn what happened when those two boats, bristling with guns, passed our leafy hideout by the river on their way to Nazareth. God was about to test Biviano's recent commitment to Himself, and strengthen him to lead others. Finding our family gone, the guerrillas went straight to Biviano's house and ordered him out. Taking him to the basketball court in the middle of the village, where everyone could see the intimidating procedure, they pushed a machine gun against his chest.

"Because of you the gringos got away. You are going to pay!" they sneered at him.

"Go ahead and shoot me," Biviano replied firmly. "I know where I am going. If you want to see blood, spill mine. It's the same as the gringos'."

They backed off and did not shoot. They had never found anyone willing to die for a cause other than their own.

God's plan for the Caño Ti through the Dulkas has been accomplished, and Biviano no longer needs a direct hand from us. But wherever we go, we recruit prayer for Biviano, Luis, Alberto and that young church: those whom Jesus has rescued from the dangerous broad river and guided into the narrow and straight creek of His love and power.